Special Places

for the discerning traveler

In

CALIFORNIA, THE PACIFIC NORTHWEST

WESTERN CANADA AND

THE NORTHERN ROCKIES

By
Fred Nystrom and Mardi Murvin Nystrom

◼ ACKNOWLEDGEMENTS

Special thanks to Chad and Tyler for their patience with their parents when we are "on the road" so often. A special welcome to Makenna Alexis who is a direct result of our being on the road, staying in these very romantic places.

◼ Special Credits

Editing: Lois Pendleton and Connie Bourassa-Shaw
Editorial assistance by Linn Hess, Nancy Hurlow and Kathryn Kincannon
Production by Common Sense Communications, Seattle, WA.

◼ Photographic Contributions

— David Barnes - 84, 85
— Don Breneman - 247, 249
— Eduardo Calderon - 151, 153
— Patrick Cudahy - 79
— Bruce Foster - 113, 115
— Mike Guryan - 235
— Don King - 119
— Michael McCurry - 61, 63, 65, 67
— Dana Olson - 147, 149
— Janet Palmer - 175, 177
— Bob Peterson - 139
— PhotoArt - 109, 111
— Doug Plummer - 73, 75, 81, 83, 91, 93, 99, 101, 117, 121, 123, 131, 137, 145, 159, 161, 163, 203, 205, 207, 211, 231, 233
— Kenneth Rice - 47, 49
— David C. Schultz- 267, 269
— Michael T. Seidl - 95, 97, 199, 201, 239, 241, 243, 245, back cover
— David Stoecklin - 237
— Bob von Norman - 77
— John Walden - 6, 7
— Randy Wells - balloon
— Art Wolfe - cover
— Joseph Woods - 55
— Rex Zjak - 107

Copyright © 1989
ISBN 0-936777-01-X
Library of Congress Number: 89-92165
Fourth edition format: Common Sense Communications
Original book design: C. Oller

Printed in U.S.A.

INTRODUCTION

Since our first edition four years ago, our concept has been to search out, by personal visits, independently owned lodging, restaurant and allied businesses who maintain a similar high level of quality, service and personal attention to the needs of their guests. While the ambiance of an urban hotel like the Bedford is different than that of a rural bed and breakfast like the Gingerbread Mansion, the level of personal caring and attention to your needs is consistently high. We do not include chains or formula restaurants.

In a concerted effort to add only those few really Special Places, we've taken the step of creating a self-monitoring Association consisting of the innkeepers and restaurateurs who were in our prior editions. These people work with us to help select the new places to be added or the hotels and restaurants to be dropped when their quality goes down. This intense, professional peer scrutiny keeps the quality of the Special Places very high, and it sets this book apart from all others.

The criteria we've established for a property to be added or dropped from the Association is exacting. Current members must ask themselves, "Would I be willing to stay there myself or to recommend this place to one of my guests?" And, "Are the people running the place highly professional in their approach?" Unless the answer to both questions is "Yes," you will not be reading about that place in this book. This double selection process ensures that you have the best travel experience possible.

During my many years with Sunset Magazine, I was always impressed with their consistent approach to presenting truthful, accurate and reliable information. We try to take that same approach and give you a written and photographic representation as close to the real experience as possible. All the copy done for this book is totally independent. The places may see a final checking copy so that any factual errors can be corrected. In this fourth edition, we are very pleased to continue to expand geographically. Our goal is to cover the thirteen western states and two provinces.

We hope you will enjoy these Special Places as much as we have. When you visit one, please say, "I found you in Special Places."

Fred and Mardi Nystrom

TABLE OF CONTENTS

California 6

Inn at Rancho Santa Fe 12
Little Inn on the Bay 16
Villa Rosa 20
The Alisal Guest Ranch 24
Erna's Elderberry House 28
The Martine Inn 30
The Babbling Brook 34
Inn at the Opera 38
The Spencer House 42
The Mansion at Lakewood 46
The Wine Country Inn 50
Napa Valley Balloons 54
The Foothill House 56
The Toll House 60
Whale Watch Inn by the Sea 64
The Stanford Inn by the Sea 68
Benbow Inn 72
The Gingerbread Mansion 76
Carter House/Hotel Carter 80

Pacific Northwest 84

Paradise Ranch Inn 90
Black Butte Ranch 94
Rock Springs Guest Ranch 98
RiverPlace Alexis Hotel 102
Genoa 106
Heron Haus 108
The Heathman Hotel 112
Columbia Gorge Hotel 116
The Shelburne Inn and
The Shoalwater Restaurant 120
Alexis Hotel Seattle 124
Rover's 128
Dominique's Place 130
The Inn at the Market 132
Adriatica 136
Cafe Juanita 138
The Herbfarm 140
Birchfield Manor 142
brusseaus in edmonds 144
Home by the Sea 146
Inn at Langley 150
Saratoga Inn 154
Turtleback Farm Inn 158
Christina's 162
Inn at Semiahmoo 164

Western Canada 168

The Bedford Hotel 174
Abigail's Hotel 178
Beaconsfield Inn 182
Chez Daniel 186
Sooke Harbour House 188
Hastings House 192
The Old House Restaurant 196
April Point Lodge 198
Park Royal Hotel 202
Corsi Trattoria 206
Bishops 208
The William Tell 210
Hatheume Lake Resort 212
Emerald Lake Lodge 216
Buffalo Mountain Lodge 220

Northern Rockies 224

River Street Inn 230
Busterback Ranch 234
Kandahar Lodge 238
Flathead Lake Lodge 242
Lone Mountain Ranch 246
Mountain Sky Guest Ranch 250
The Wort Hotel 254
Spring Creek Resort 258
The Brigham Street Inn 262
The Homestead 266

Special Interest Indexes 270

To Reorder 272

Please help 272

California

California is the legendary Golden State because much of its history has been shaped by the eruption of greed known as the Gold Rush. What began as a myth and the Spaniards determination to find a country of gold, followed by the actual discovery of the coveted prize in 1849, resulted in the shaping of an entire state.

The first inhabitants of the state were Native Americans — thousands of small groups with distinct customs and languages. For nearly 1,000 years Indians enjoyed the bounties of the sea and the land, and had a relatively quiet life. The 16th century brought the first Europeans to Alta California, first Sir Francis Drake, then an influx of Spaniards seeking gold to mine and perhaps a few souls to save. The Indian culture was essentially crushed by the Spanish and Anglo oppression. Missions from those early attempts at conversion are still found throughout the state. In the early 1800s, when Mexico declared its independence from Spain, Mexicans settled across the border, lured by the promise of free land and the hope of discovering veins of gold rumored to be deep in the hills. For nearly five decades the *ranchero,* or cattle ranch, was the symbol of the new California, until the gold myth was brought to life and the face of the state took on a different complexion.

During the first three years of the great Gold Rush, more than 200,000 men, plus a few women and children, came across the Sierra Nevada range in one of the greatest mass migrations in history.

Diverse Regions

California may be just one state but it is made up of many different states of mind. These relate to the geographic diversity of the state. The North Coast is a very traditional area with its 400-mile ribbon of jagged headlands. Here small farms and old barns, grazing cows and wandering deer share the rolling grass lands. This is perhaps the best area in the state for long walks, quiet retreats and intimate romantic times.

The "Wine Country" of Napa and Sonoma is internationally acclaimed for its large concentration of wineries and their highly regarded products. Once beyond the sniffing, swilling and sampling, you will find an area that pulses to the seasonal demands of farming.

The cosmopolitan San Francisco Bay area with its nearly 6 million residents, has "The City" as its focus. The performing arts, street performers, fine arts and local crafts, ethnic cuisine and local seafood all find room to thrive in lively San Francisco.

Still considered as part of Northern California, the area around the Monterey Peninsula is universally acclaimed for its natural beauty. From Santa Cruz to Big Sur, this is an area of breathtaking seascapes and charming towns.

Santa Barbara and the areas to the north still feel like old California during the quieter years before the waves of migration changed it all. The red tile roofs, the Channel Islands just off shore and the surrounding hills all help to cloister Santa Barbara from the urban sprawl to the south.

Los Angeles, known as the "City of Angels," will soon overtake New York for the dubious honor of being the nation's most populated area.

The Orange County beach communities, starting with Newport Beach and stretching south to San Diego are fun to explore. Funky and disheveled to ritzy and expensive, the coastal drive will expose you to the gambit.

San Diego has the beaches and the border. Some of the charm of old California and some of the growth problems of Los Angeles. The beauty of Rancho Santa Fe and the dreariness of endless stucco suburbs. For years, getting dressed up in San Diego meant wearing new shorts and a fresh t-shirt. Now the arts and cultural activities are well supported and flourishing.

The Best Times to Visit

Due to the large population and the influx of summer visitors, the trick to enjoying California is to come after schools start. Travel is much more enjoyable from late September to May. Because of the inland heat, June seems to be universally foggy all along the coast.

Border Crossings

The State Department of Food and Agriculture has established inspection stations along all roads entering California. All produce, plant materials and animals are subject to inspection. To avoid delays, do not transport any agricultural products into the state.

Liquor Laws

The legal drinking age in California is 21. Liquor is sold by the bottle or can in liquor stores and supermarkets. Alcoholic beverages are sold by the drink in most restaurants and bars from 6 a.m. to 2 a.m.

Information Sources for California

California Office of Tourism
1121 L Street, Suite 103
Sacramento, CA 95814
Catalogue order desk: (800) 862-2543

SAN DIEGO

NEWPORT
BEACH

LOS ANGELES

SANTA BARBARA

SOLVANG

SAN SIMEON

MONTEREY
CARMEL

SANTA
CRUZ

SAN FRANCISCO
OAKLAND
NAPA

MENDOCINO
GUALALA

GARBERVILLE

FERNDALE
EUREKA

REDDING

SACRAMENTO

YOSEMITE
NAT'L PARK

FRESNO

CALIFORNIA SPECIAL PLACES

A Inn at Rancho Santa Fe

B Little Inn on The Bay

C Villa Rosa

D The Alisal Guest Ranch

E Erma's Elderberry House

F The Martine Inn

G The Babbling Brook

H Inn at The Opera

I Spencer House

J Mansion at Lakewood

K Wine Country Inn

L Napa Valley Balloons

M Foothill House

N Toll House

O Whale Watch Inn

P Stanford Inn

Q Benbow Inn

R Gingerbread Mansion

S Carter House and Hotel Carter

INN AT RANCHO SANTA FE

Address:	P.O. Box 869, Rancho Santa Fe, CA 92067
Telephone:	(619) 756-1131
	(800) 654-2928, room reservations only
Location:	On Lomas Santa Fe Drive, seven miles from I-5 in the Village of Rancho Santa Fe
Host:	Daniel Royce, Innkeeper
Room Rates:	$85 to $165 double; $235 to $460 suites and private cottages
Credit Cards:	All major
Remarks:	Children welcome. No pets. European and American plan conference rates available.

For present day residents, the small town of Rancho Santa Fe captures the essence of California. Spanish colonial homes with red-tiled roofs built amid groves of eucalyptus trees form this planned community. But for Juan Osuna, what used to be known as Rancho San Diequito was nothing but a dry, barren land. His happiest day was when he unloaded his burden to the Santa Fe railroad for $12.00 an acre.

The railroad purchased the 8,824-acre parcel to begin an experiment in growing eucalyptus trees for railroad ties. They planted some 3,000,000 seedlings. The project was abandoned due to the unsuitability of the wood. The eucaplyptus were left to flourish and the railroad converted the remaining unplanted acreage into citrus agriculture and residential development—one of California's earliest planned communities. Today the area is an aesthetic blend of eucalyptus trees, citrus groves and beautiful homesites. Horse paddocks and lush green golf courses complete the picture.

Cultivated Rusticity

The Inn at Rancho Santa Fe fits perfectly into this cultivated rusticity. The La Morada Guest House, part of the inn's main building, was built in 1923 to accommodate prospective land buyers. In 1941, George Richardson purchased the inn with plans to develop it into a quiet resort. He added cottages and landscaped gardens. The Royce family bought the property in 1958. Through three generations, they have maintained the ranchos tradition of considering each guests individual needs. The ambience is relaxed, but luxurious. This level of care has created a very loyal following.

The Cottages

Seventeen one-story cottages stud the 20 acres of landscaped grounds. Each cottage has two to ten individual guest bedrooms. All of the 75 rooms and suites are light and airy with cozy, contemporary furnishings. Some include fireplaces, kitchens and wet bars. Some have lanais. All have private entrances and baths, separately air-conditioned bedrooms, comfortable patios and private parking within a few yards. For families, connecting rooms can be made into two-room suites. There are also a number of one and two-bedroom cottages adjacent to the inn, with full hotel services available.

The inn's spacious lobby is furnished with family antiques and an astonishing collection of model sailing vessels. Comfortable furnishings are situated around an impressive brick fireplace.

Three championship tennis courts are reserved for guests to use. The inn does not have its own golf course, but membership is maintained at two private 18-hole courses ensuring convenient and available tee times for guests. For those looking for beach time, the inn maintains a cottage complete with showers, dressing rooms and a private patio on the beach at nearby Del Mar.

In addition to plenty of recreation and relaxation, the inn offers a selection of dining rooms with a variety of menus. The Garden Room, overlooking the pool, is open for breakfast, lunch, dinner and Sunday brunch. The Vintage Room, a replica of an old California taproom, is perfect for cocktails, lunch or dinner. Set within the perimeter of floor-to-ceiling bookcases, the Library tastefully combines culinary with intellectual pursuits. The Patio Room makes for delightful alfresco dining. During the summer months, the Patio Terrace features dancing under the stars on Friday and Saturday nights. Room service is available during regular dining hours. Beverages are available in the Vintage Room or from room service from 11:00 a.m. to 11:00 p.m.

Rancho Rambling

Rancho Santa Fe is in the heart of San Diego's north county. It is a region famous for fruit and nut orchards. The farm-grown produce is so good, chefs from Los Angeles often drive down to personally select from the fields.

San Diego is nearby, and Mexico only and hour away. Nearby attractions include Sea World in Mission Bay, Balboa Park, the San Diego Zoo and the Wild Animal Park. August and September is horseracing season at Del Mar. The front desk can provide information on these and other attractions. The Inn holds a box at the races and may have seats available for guests.

Rancho Santa Fe is inland just enough to avoid the coastal fogs that can make for chilly June days all along the California coast.

Croquet is frequently played by local clubs.

Corporate Retreat

The inn has a special crew with the sole responsibility of handling meeting preparation. The Meeting House, a specially designed conference building that seats 100, can be subdivided into three independent "break out" rooms. It is air-conditioned, well-lighted and equipped for audio-visual projection. The inn has other fully-equipped comfortable meeting rooms to host smaller groups up to 25. For conference meals and entertaining, the inn can provide private rooms and hospitality suites.

Getting There

The inn is located just twenty-five miles north of San Diego. Transportation can be arranged from Lindbergh Field or the Santa Fe Station in Del Mar. By car, take I-5 north from San Diego or south from Los Angeles. Exit at Lomas Santa Fe Drive. Continue east five miles to the Village of Rancho Santa Fe when the street changes to Linea del Cielo. The inn is on the left, just before the Village.

LITTLE INN ON THE BAY

Address:	617 Lido Park Drive, Newport Beach, CA 92663
Telephone:	(714) 673-8800; (800) 438-4466 toll-free in California; (800) 538-4466 toll-free nationwide
Hosts:	Herrick and Janice Hanson, Owners
Room Rates:	$96.00 double; $135 to $160 suites
Credit Cards:	All major
Remarks:	Two-night minimum on weekends mid-June to mid-September. No pets.

Imagine a harbor of calm within a hurricane of commercialized activity. An oasis of tranquility. A refuge of relaxation and solitude. The slow-paced, New England charm of The Little Inn on the Bay provides welcome insulation from the fast-living of a southern California beach city.

The 19th-century nautical setting is real enough to conjure up the smell of an old sea captain's pipe tobacco. The New England-style hospitality makes families, lovers, foreign guests and businessmen alike feel at home.

A Taste of Cape Cod

When Herrick and Janice Hanson purchased the neighborhood hotel in 1979, they knew it was special. Newport Beach has six miles of wide sandy beaches as well as twenty-five miles of shoreline in its harbor. However, there are very few accommodations near the water. The Little Inn on the Bay was and still is the only hotel property located right on the water in Newport Beach. The Hansons began a two-year renovation in 1986. With a pocketful of dreams and hearts full of memories about growing up in a 200-year-old Delaware farmhouse, the Hansons transformed the ugly-duckling property into a beautiful 30-room inn of comfortable elegance and New England authenticity.

The renovation entailed an entire gutting of the property. The Hansons kept the inn open during the two-year renovation process with only minimal discomfort to their guests. In fact, the guests entered into the spirit of the transformation, offering suggestions. Since then, many have returned to experience the results.

Each room and suite is individually and authentically designed and decorated to convey the feel of a New England sea coast inn during the early 1800's. From crown mouldings to draperies and bedspreads, handmade candle sconces and soid brass Baldwin lamps to authentic color schemes— the Little Inn has created a very special environment for visitors to Newport Beach.

Their goal of combining Cape Cod charm with contemporary amenities has been achieved. Each room and suite is decorated with slightly different detail. The eight bay-front suites afford a panoramic view of Newport Harbor. Each has a king-size bed, large living area, and wet bar with a refrigerator and microwave oven. Four channel suites feature king-size beds, a wet bar and refrigerator, and views in two directions: the bay and the Rhine Channel, with a working dock for fishing boats. The fifteen deluxe queen rooms are well-appointed and comfortable, three are perfect for family accommodations.

The "creature comforts" at The Little Inn on the Bay make a stay there a wonderful, indulgent experience. A paper is at each door in the morning. A continental breakfast of pastries and freshly brewed coffee are served in the lobby. As a thirst quencher in the afternoon, sun tea is available by the pool. Wine, cheese and hors d'oeuvres are offered in the lobby each evening between six and seven p.m. And for guests of any age, freshly-baked chocolate chip cookies and milk are available before retiring for the night.

The friendly interaction among the guests is a big part of the Little Inn's spirit. The guests have the opportunity to gather in the lobby at the end of the day to discuss favorite places to dine. There are over thirty restaurants within walking distance of the inn.

Aside from the special touches, the Hansons believe "it is our staff that brings people back." They take care of the special extras that make guests feel pampered and comfortable. When guests from outside of the States arrive, the flags of their countries are flown throughout their stay.

Sun, Fun, Shopping

The inn is but a stone's throw away from Lido Island, and walking distance to more than 30 restaurants. It has its own marina and a launch for evening harbor cruises. A fleet of bicycles is available for the spontaneous adventurer who might want to bike down to the beach. The staff has put together four walking tours and a bycycle tour that invite exploration of the old Newport area. Or for the less ambitious, the peddling can be left to an experienced pedicab chauffeur who will narrate a jaunt through the village streets.

For those who have time to venture farther, Disneyland and Knott's Berry Farm are less than an hour's drive from the inn. Fashion Island and the South Coast Plaza are not far for those who would rather be shopping. The activity list offers plenty of other choices too: fishing, boating, golf, horseback riding, roller skating, or spectating with other fans at Dodger Stadium.

If a day in the sun is on the agenda and the attitude is "when in Rome, do as the Romans do," there are miles of wide, sandy beach on which to lanquidly

The rooms face the water and moorage.

soak in the rays. The inn's outdoor pool offers a comfortable perch from which to watch sleek yachts and sassy sailboats out in the harbor and get some sun.

The inn makes a delightful place to host small meetings. Twenty-five can be easily accommodated in a specially arranged Bay Front Suite.

Getting There

The inn is twelve miles south of the John Wayne/Orange County Airport, and approximately forty miles from the Los Angeles International Airport.
By car, take Highway 55 (the Newport Freeway) until it ends, becoming Newport Boulevard. Follow Newport Boulevard about five miles, past the Pacific Coast Highway. Turn left on 32nd Street. Go one block. Turn right on Lafayette. Go one block. Turn left onto Lido Park Drive. The inn is a half block up on the left, just opposite the Cannery Restaurant.

VILLA ROSA

Address:	15 Chapala, Santa Barbara, CA 93101
Telephone:	(805) 966-0851
Host:	Beverly Kirkhart, Owner/Innkeeper
Room Rates:	$90 to $185 double. Two-night minimum on weekends and holidays.
Credit Cards:	American Express, MasterCard, Visa
Remarks:	Rates include continental breakfast, complimentary wine and cheese, evening port and sherry. Children over 14 welcome. No pets.

Blue ocean views from private verandas, palm trees, avocado groves and a sensual evening breeze make the Villa Rosa an enchanted place that is woven into the colorful tapestry of Santa Barbara.

Immediately upon entering Santa Barbara, you are aware that this is no ordinary beach town. The thing that sets the different cast is the architecture. The thick adobe walls with deeply recessed doors and windows, the graceful balconies and loggias and the red tiled roofs are all reminiscent of villages along Spains Mediterranean coast. Perhaps this should be expected since Santa Barbara was under Spanish and Mexican control from 1782 until 1846. However there is little left from that period. The migrating Anglos hated the Spanish architecture and tore down most of the old buildings and a typical Western town, heavily Victorian, took their place. After the 1925 earthquake the Architectural Board of Review decided to promote the Spanish Colonial look which can now be seen and appreciated throughout the town.

Preserving the Past

In keeping with the preservation spirit many of the centrally located historic hotels are being restored to their former elegance. The Spanish Colonial Revival Villa Rosa was built in 1931 and known for years as The Hilton-by-the-Sea. During its many years the building was used as an apartment house, a motel and as off campus housing for the students at UCSB. The decline in fortunes for the building continued until Mark and Beverly Kirkhart accepted the challenge and purchased the 9,000-square foot building in 1981.

Transforming the dilapidated waterfront motel into an immaculate and elegant 18-room inn was no easy feat. The total interior was gutted, the foundation was rehabilitated and a completely new roof installed. Mark's architectural creativity continued as he enclosed the courtyard, added a solar heated pool and jacuzzi and created space for small meetings. Beverly's decorating skills

came to play in furnishing the rooms in a Spanish Colonial style with a contemporary flair of the Southwest.

Mark and Beverly's restoration and the hospitality the guests now receive has made the Villa Rosa a success story to be envied by anyone with similar innkeeping aspirations.

Villa Perfecta

The affectionate pseudonym "Villa Perfecta" aptly describes this romantic retreat that is steeped in sophisticated elegance. Guests who stay receive a range of amenities that would be found in a first class European resort and the personalized pampering of a domestic bed and breakfast inn.

The pale pink, two-story building presents a facade of visual diversity: turreted corners, cupolas, arched porticos and wrought iron balconies. Spectacular views of the beach, Stearns Wharf and mountains lining the south coast are rewarding sights from the inside. In typical Spanish tradition, there is also a serene garden courtyard complete with spa and pool.

There is an instant sense of belonging as guests are greeted into the living room by Beverly or one of her staff. A few moments in front of the magnificent fireplace with a mug of freshly brewed coffee or a refreshing glass of wine may introduce thoughts of never leaving.

The rooms are decorated with Spanish and Mexican art and exotic potted plants. The terracotta-tiled baths add to the Mediterranean feel. Terry robes are an amenity that make lounging a necessity. The villa's signature rose graces the pillow on your turned down bed each evening. Three suites include small kitchen facilities ideal for longer stays. Four deluxe rooms feature fireplaces and sitting areas ideal for relaxing with a good book. All rooms have telephones. TVs are available on request.

Flair without Fanfare

A complimentary breakfast of croissants, muffins, fruit and freshly brewed coffee is served in the sitting room. Room or poolside service can be arranged by special request. Wine, cheese and social congenialities can be found in the living room from 5 to 7 p.m.

The Villa Rosa staff is available to help with dinner reservations and information about local attractions. They are also happy to make appointments with the inn's masseuse.

The recently completed conference room is an ideal site for small workshops and executive retreats. It offers professional conveniences in a quiet setting.

The courtyard privacy is only eighty-four steps to the beach.

High Energy or Relaxation

Santa Barbara is currently in the midst of a spirited revival of the cultivated arts. Always a big music town, the talk now likens it to a "little Salzburg." It is also home to California's oldest continually running cinema house—the Lobero Theater. Take a trolley ride to the Mission, the zoo or an historic museum. Or, rent a bike and follow the coastline. Perhaps it's the perfect time to don a linen suit for "high tea" at the classic Biltmore. Be it active or passive, Santa Barbara offers choices that appeal to both.

Getting There

Traveling south, from Highway 101, turn west at Chapala by the big fig tree. Cross the railroad tracks and watch for Villa Rosa on your right, one block from Cabrillo Boulevard (which runs along the ocean). Traveling north, take Highway 101 to the Cabrillo Blvd. exit. Turn left at the stop sign. Follow Cabrillo Blvd. to Chapala Street. Villa Rosa is on the left.

THE ALISAL GUEST RANCH

Address:	1054 Alisal Road, Solvang, CA 93463
Telephone:	(805) 688-6411
Host:	Jack Austin, General Manager
Room Rates:	$205 studio; $255 2-room suite; $450 private bungalow with 3 bedrooms and 2 baths. Rates based on double occupancy. Two night minimum. Special packages available from September to June.
Credit Cards:	MasterCard, Visa
Remarks:	All rooms have woodburning fireplaces. No pets, bicycles or skateboards. Rates include breakfast and dinner.

Surrounded by gently rolling hills that are golden in the summer and emerald green with splashes of wildflowers in the spring, the Alisal Guest Ranch is nestled in the secluded Santa Ynez Valley. The ranch's 10,000 acres are generously populated with eagles, hawks, deer, and occasional coyotes and mountain lion. Huge century-old live oaks dot the hillsides. But it is the sycamores that gave the place its name. In Chumash, Alisal means "grove of sycamores." The native Americans named the area after the number of sycamores that they found in the secluded valley.

Under Spanish rule, the ranch was one of four original land grants in the region. Today, the Alisal remains largely intact from the original 13,000-acre grant made to Jose Raimundo Carrillo around 1782. Carrillo's brand, over 250 years old, is still used on the property's livestock and as the ranch's logo.

The present owners, the Jackson family, acquired the Alisal in 1943. It soon became popular as a family gathering place, and a getaway for corporate executives and entertainment celebrities. The Jacksons have continued the tradition of California ranch life. They maintain the property as a working cattle ranch where some 2,000 calves are fattened each winter.

Luxurious Retreat

Only forty miles north of Santa Barbara, the Alisal guest ranch is not a dude ranch where visitors participate in chores, but rather a luxurious retreat that captures the feeling of living on a large, working ranch. It occupies about 350 acres of the land and can accommodate about 200 guests.

Guest cottages are clustered around manicured lawns, and are decorated in simple motifs that reflect the ranch heritage. Bungalows that line the entrance

have front porches, two and three bedrooms and large living rooms. Studios and two-room suites can be arranged for either king or twin beds. All have working fireplaces. TVs and telephones are limited to the recreation cabin and a few pay phones scattered around the property.

An exciting addition to the Alisal's fully-equipped conference facility is a beautiful 1,500-square foot Hospitality House. It features a central livingroom suite, surrounded by three separate studio rooms—all with private entrances.

Fun and Frivolity

A ride into oak-studded hills will tempt even the slickest of the city slickers. The tack room is equipped with polished bridles and managed by ranch hands that have a repetoire of entertaining stories. Two-hour guided trail rides are scheduled each morning and afternoon. Lessons are available for novice riders. Trail dust can be washed off with a dip in the large, free-form pool.

There is a 6,286-yard, par 72 golf course that was designed by Billy Bell. It utilizes the natural terrain, the sycamores and the live oaks to create a challenging championship course. A resident PGA pro is on staff to assist guests in reducing their handicaps or improving their swing. There is a fully-equipped pro shop and lounge to make the package complete. It isn't necessary to book tee off times since the course is reserved exclusively for ranch guests and a few private members.

Seven championship tennis courts and a pro shop comprise the tennis center. The resident teaching pro and assistants are there to assist and arrange tournaments. Lessons are enhanced by videotaped analysis.

The Alisal even has its own 100-acre lake. In addition to sailing, rowing and windsurfing, guests can go fishing. The lake is stocked with bluegill, catfish and largemouth bass. Since the lake is on private land, there is no license requirement. Tackle is supplied to guests.

Counselor-directed activities are available for children during the summer months. Craft projects, hikes and scavenger hunts give the younger crowd plenty of memories to take home with them. Volleyball contests and croquet tournaments are regular activities.

Rest and Relaxation

In the evenings, guests can relax by the fire in their rooms, or enjoy the fireplace in the library. The recreation room has a pool table, games and sports a casual restaurant and bar.

Dining at the Alisal is in keeping with real ranch life. Chef Scott Douglass concentrates on quality and quantity. Nouvelle has taken a back seat to good,

There is always room to relax in front of the fire.

hearty meals. Steak and prime rib are features on the menu. But to keep things interesting, there are always a few dishes prepared with fresh local seafood from Santa Barbara. Lamb salad with fresh herbs is also an offering. The kitchen turns out wonderful desserts everyday including homemade ice creams. Each week, there are outdoor cookouts and breakfast rides.

Summer is peak season at the ranch when families book for a week or more. But the beauty of the hills in spring and the trees in the fall make visiting Alisal special anytime of the year.

Alisal is located near the picture-book town of Solvang, a charming little Danish community with restaurants, shops and services.

Getting There

Airline service is available to Santa Barbara forty miles away with limousine service to the ranch. By car, take Highway 101 to the Solvang/Lompoc exit. Go east through Buellton for three miles to Solvang. Right on Alisal Road, past the golf course to Alisal's main entrance.

ERNA'S ELDERBERRY HOUSE

Address:	P.O. Box 2413, Oakhurst, CA 93644
Telephone:	(209) 683-6800
Host:	Erna Kubin, Owner/Chef
Cuisine:	California regional with a European flair
Prices:	Six-course prix fixe dinner, $38 to $42; lunch, $15; Sunday brunch, $16.50.
Credit Cards:	MasterCard, Visa
Hours:	Dinner: Wednesday through Monday, 5:30-8:30; Lunch: Wednesday through Friday, 11:30-1:00; Sunday brunch: 11:00-5:00. Closed Tuesdays. Reservations required.

The Elderberry House is a dining experience of culinary and artistic mastery. It has received high critical acclaim for its hospitality and warmth. "One of the most elegant and stylish restaurants in the nation, " is how Craig Claiborne describes La Domaine du Sureau also know as Erna's Elderberry House. Yet despite any hint of folksiness gleaned from its name or its location on the fringes of Yosemite National Park, the Elderberry House is, as Claiborne discerned, the masterpiece of an exceptionally talented Viennese woman.

A Dining Destination

"I have the simplest of tastes," reads the plaque over the Elderberry kitchen. "I want only the best." As you revel in the Old World charm of the house, it is evident that Erna is true to her word. A wrought iron gate admits you to a seven-acre hilltop setting, crowned with a 5,500 square foot Mediterranean-style building of white stucco and red tile. Nestled amid mature elderberry bushes, rustic oaks and sugar pines, the terrain is the hear and soul of Erna's French Provence.

Trained in art and design in London, New York and Los Angeles, Kubin's style is displayed everywhere. Four individual dining rooms, three named after culinary mentors Auguste Escoffier, Fernand Point, Paul Bocuse, and a slate rock wine cellar bar are the result of an artist's loving hand.

The main dining room, the Escoffier, has elegant, high beamed ceilings draped with ornate brass chandeliers. Tapestries of pastoral scenes and period oils add the finishing touch to a room filled with striped silk chairs and tables appointed in damask linen. The Point, with a light and airy French country feel, features stylish whitewashed furnishings covered in pretty Provencal prints.

The overture of a meal at the Elderberry House is a flute of the house aperitif, a "sureau" of champagne and elderberry nectar. The grand finale is a delectable dessert such as a warm Viennese "apfel strudel" or local wild cherries served with a praline terrine.

In between you'll find five delicious dishes beautifully presented. She uses only the choices seasonal ingredients, and everything is prepared fresh in the Elderberry House kitchen. The entree, accompanied by the house's signature palette of seven fresh vegetables, may be tender pork loin stuffed with fresh apricots and plums in a caraway beer sauce with wild rice one night, broiled medallions of venison, a savory chocolate-cinnamon sauce and walnut past the next. There are always options should a guest prefer something other than the selected entree, and the wait staff is fully capable of suggesting the perfect accompaniment from an extensive list of California and European vintages.

Getting There

The Elderberry House is three hours north of Los Angeles and the same distance east from San Francisco. It is thirty minutes south of Yosemite's south entrance and one and one-half hours from Yosemite Valley. Take Highway 41 north from Fresno about forty minutes, through Coarsegold, up and over a steep grade. Before reaching the bottom, take the left hand turn lane with a "Sierra Meadows Emergency Care Unit" sign at its corner, onto Victoria Lane, which leads directly through the restaurant gates.

This French auberge on the way to Yosemite.

THE MARTINE INN

Address:	255 Oceanview Boulevard, Pacific Grove, CA 93950
Telephone:	(408) 373-3388
Hosts:	Don and Marion Martine
Room Rates:	$99 to $205 double, includes breakfast
Credit Cards:	MasterCard, Visa
Remarks:	No children under 16, no pets, smoking in fireplace rooms only.

The Monterey Peninsula spans the rocky coastline beginning just 120 miles south of San Francisco. Its hub is the town of Monterey, a cradle of history for Northern California. Native Indians, Spanish conquerors, Mexican ranchers and American settlers have at various times passed through and played their roles in the unfolding plot. Author John Steinbeck depicted the fishing community in his mid-1940's novel "Cannery Row." The area around the original sardine cannery is now a labyrinth of shops, galleries and eateries. Just three blocks from this vital area, where Monterey meets Pacific Grove along the scenic Oceanview Boulevard, is the Martine Inn.

The Martine Inn is a gracious bed and breakfast overlooking Monterey Bay. Built in 1899, the original home was true Victorian. It was owned for many years by the Parke family of Parke Davis Pharmaceuticals, who converted it to a Mediterranean-fashioned villa. The Martine family purchased the home in 1972, and Marion and Don fully renovated it in keeping with the Victorian traditions. "We want our guests to feel as though they are visiting the home as the guests of the Parke's would have at the turn of the century," says Marion.

Complete Suites

In renovating the inn, the Martine's took particular care with details. Inlaid oak and mahogany floors were lovingly restored, and the wall coverings and paint carefully selected in keeping with the era. Each of the 19 rooms is individually decorated to reveal a unique character. Elegant museum quality antiques carry out the theme. The Martines have searched extensively for complete bedroom suites for each room, and have unearthed some interesting finds. The Edith Head room contains her own bedroom suite, as well as a commissioned portrait; the McClatchy suite is furnished from the estate of C.K. McClatchy; the Park room features a 1860 Chippendale Revival four poster bed, complete with canopy and side curtains. The Oriental Room boasts an authentic Oriental wedding bed, graced with hand painted panels and beveled glass. The Art Deco room's decor is accented by a lit Coca Cola sign, while the Pewter Room is so in character that even its light fixtures are pewter.

Ocean Views

Thirteen of the rooms have a wood burning fireplace, wood provided of course. Many have an ocean view, and all have private bath. Two oceanside parlor areas were provided by the Martines, so even those without view rooms may enjoy the water vista. An enclosed, landscaped courtyard offers a quiet spot for reading, and there is a conference room available for meetings. The 1870's steam bath and hot tub add to your relaxation. For fun and games visit the game room with its 1890's billiard table and nickelodeon. Pull Don to the side and ask to see his MG collection and find out how he did recently racing one of his prize antique cars. Finishing touches are being applied to the glass enclosed pool room, jacuzzi and steam bath just added off the courtyard.

Elegant Service

The oceanside dining room contains an impressive collection of silver and china, all carefully selected by Don and Marion. Most of it is used daily. A 1765 Old Sheffield server, Victorian condiment and pickle service, and signed Tiffany loving cups are but a few of the treasures to be found in the cupboards. Antique china service is used for breakfast, and coffee is served in individual Victorian silver pots.

In the evening, as twilight spreads across the California coast, guests of the Martine Inn gather for hors d'oeuvres and a glass of wine in the parlor. While a fire warms the room, guests sample an array of appetizers from stuffed mushrooms to puff pastry with a proscuitto, honey, and mustard filling.

Breakfast at the Martine Inn is a meal not to be missed. The inn's chef prepares fresh and wonderful creations such as crab Benedict, salmon Wellington or Spanish egg bake. Fresh fruit, juice and homemade breads accompany the meal. The full-time chef is available to cater the many weddings, meetings and other functions often held at the inn.

On the Peninsula

The Martine Inn enjoys a prime location on the Monterey Peninsula within easy walking distance of many attractions. The Monterey Aquarium is just a few blocks from the inn, and features nearly one hundred innovative habitat galleries and exhibits. Visitors experience Monterey Bay on a journey into its deep reefs and turbulent tide pools. Monterey's historic Fisherman's Wharf houses a large fishing fleet, and it, too, has its share of shops and seafood restaurants. A walking tour of historic Monterey, called the Path of History, winds past the Fisherman's Wharf on its route through the city's important sites. The self-guide tour includes public buildings, ancient adobe structures, and other significant sites where history was made. A favorite walk in Pacific Grove is the Victorian tour, which takes you past homes of the 1800s.

This is a perfect room for winter storm watching.

The staff at the inn is dedicated to creating a pleasurable, well-rounded experience for the guest. They are able to arrange golf and tennis games, bike rentals, and suggest local dining establishments. The inn's library is stocked with literature on nearby attractions as well as menus from most restaurants.

Some of the finest sites of the Monterey Bay area may be seen from the comfort of the Martine Inn. Winter is the best time to watch for migrating whales, but year-round otters and seals play in the surf, and seabirds feed along the shore right in front of the door.

Getting There

From Highway 1, take the Pacific Grove/Pebble Beach turnoff. Follow signs on Highway 68 to Pacific Grove. The road becomes Forest Avenue. Stay in the right lane all the way to Ocean View Boulevard. Take a right and proceed fifteen blocks to the inn. Private parking is available.

THE BABBLING BROOK

Address:	1025 Laurel Street, Santa Cruz, CA 95060
Telephone:	(408) 427-2437
Host:	Helen King
Room Rates:	$85 to $125, double occupancy. Includes full country breakfast and afternoon wine and cheese.
Credit Cards:	American Express, Discover, MasterCard, Visa
Remarks:	Children over 12 welcome. No pets.

To the eye of Van Gogh or Degas,, life was more than the sum of its parts. Within their surreal canvases of sweeping brushstrokes and delicate daubs, stories unfolded in a single landscape, figures flowed as if in a dream, brilliant colors left impressions to enrich the soul and endure the test of time.

The "joie de vivre" of these painters lives on at The Babbling Brook Inn in sunny Santa Cruz today, not only through the beauty of their prints which adorn the guest rooms that bear their names, but in the aesthetic blending of past with present, the artistic balance of nature and modern amenities. The world Helen King has carefully nurtured with love and appreciation.

An Historic Masterpiece

Beside The Babbling Brook's cascading waterfall lies an ancient Ohlone Indian burial grounds. Artifacts from the protected archaeological dig site continue to emerge. The property subsequently hosted an 18 century grist mill run by Mission fathers and a tannery, complete with water wheel, during the Gold Rush days. It was the haunt of the Russian czar's last United States representative, and the creative haven for Jesse Grant, Ulysses's son, who lived there while writing his father's biography.

In 1924, Charles Chandler and his wife turned the property into a Roaring 20's retreat. Mrs. Chandler, who aspired to the role of high society hostess, had an upstairs built onto the existing log cabin, stone retaining walls, an enormous wine press, an outdoor stone bread oven and rotisserie, and elaborate gardens. Lloyd Wright bought the home in 1942 as a restaurant, christening it "The Babbling Brook." The Babbling Brook Inn opened as the first Santa Cruz bed and breakfast inn in 1981.

Garden of Earthly Delights

A small handcrafted sign greets you as you step onto the inn's front deck: "Time began in a garden." That's easy to believe here... Tree-sized fuchsias and laurels bend and sway in the breeze, wildflowers carpet the hillsides, ferns poke through nooks and crannies, and a stately old redwood offers shade to every visitor. A vintage covered bridge adds a touch of Old World elegance and, above it all, you can hear the sound of the waterfall, which flows gracefully around the cottages.

Every guestroom in the shingled cottages commands a romantic view of the hillside, overlooking gardens and brook. Each room and suite has its own country French flair by the colors and paintings associated with a particular Impressionist artist. Soothing pastels and touches of delft blue are accented with bouquets of freshly cut wildflowers, Laura Ashley linens and embroidered comforters spread over king and queen beds. French doors open onto private balconies and all but two rooms have woodburning fireplaces. Those without can enjoy the warmth of a deep jet bathtub. The Honeymoon Suite has a large antique bathtub and canopied bed, stained glass windows, skylights and outside entrance.

The comfortable living room is filled with soft chairs and cozy sofas. You can sit by the roaring fire playing backgammon or cards, doze to the soothing piano music in the background or read through Helen's restaurant book, in which guests have written their reviews of more than 100 restaurants.

Helen's Breakfast

Under a skylit atrium, charming breakfast tables await their morning guests. A breakfast at Babbling Brook is no ordinary experience. Helen, whose cooking has won awards as well as accolades from family and guests, presents a buffet of homemade croissants, a variety of muffins, wholesome granola and wonderful coffee and juices. A tea tray filled with her cookies rests in the foyer. You'll find wine and cheese to greet you when you return from an afternoon of boardwalk strolling or beach town browsing.

The Babbling Brook Inn is made even more inviting by the domestic touches of a mother's pride. Helen King welcomes her guests as she would her family, with kindness, warmth and happiness. Expertly attending to even the smallest details, she is a gracious and attentive hostess. A visit to the inn is as comfortable as a trip home – the serene surroundings, the magic of nature's splashing colors create a dramatic yet restful portrait.

Sights and Sounds of Santa Cruz

An engaging Bohemian throwback to the surf cities of yesteryear, Santa Cruz maintains a refreshingly "happy go lucky" air. Surfers peddle by dragging

The living room is a place for breakfast and conversation.

their boards. Early morning docks are lined with fishermen drinking strong coffee and predicting the day's forecast. And the music of the Boardwalk's carousel reminds you that this is a setting made for beach blanket bingo. You'll find the shops, galleries and restaurants of Capitola Village and Soquel Avenue filled with the creations of innovative artists.

Fall brings the whales to nearby Año Nuevo State Park and the Monarch butterflies to beautifully Natural Bridges Beach Park. The University of California at Santa Cruz offers a variety of dramatic and musical events. Their Shakespeare Festival is touted as one of the best.

Getting There

From the north, take Highway 17 to Highway 1, toward Half Moon Bay. Follow Highway 1 into Santa Cruz and turn left on Laurel Street. The inn will be a couple of blocks down on your right. From the south, take Highway 1 two blocks into town to Laurel Street. Turn right two blocks toward the ocean. The inn will be on your right.

INN AT THE OPERA

Address: 333 Fulton Street, San Francisco, CA 94102
Telephone: (415) 863-8400
Host: Annabella Wisniewski, General Manager
Room Rates: $105 to $140, Double; Suites $155 to $195
Credit Cards: American Express, Diners Club, MasterCard, Visa
Remarks: Children welcome. Rates include Continental breakfast served in the Act IV Restaurant.

UNDER NEW MANAGEMENT — NO LONGER RECOMMENDED

San Francisco has long been a favorite travel destination. Recently, many of the interesting older hotel and commercial buildings have been remodeled into well furnished alternatives to the large downtown highrise hotels. It is now possible to stay in "the city" and not have to stay in the downtown business core area.

San Francisco is a city of neighborhoods. One of the most vital and creative is the Civic Center, an area rich with the city's major governmental and arts complexes. The cluster of eight buildings around the perimeter of the Civic Center Plaza are said to be the "architecturally grandest in the country." Just one block away is the Inn at the Opera.

Built in 1927 and operated as the Alden Hotel, the Inn at the Opera has a unique history of catering to visiting opera stars, conductors, musicians and upcoming artists. Totally renovated in 1985 under new ownership, the luxury hotel continues to serve many artists and patrons, as well as out-of-town visitors and San Francisco residents.

Full-Service Hotel

Inn at the Opera has 48 rooms on seven floors. Eighteen are suites. Each room features a queen-size bed, fully stocked wet bar and refrigerator, and a microwave oven. Designer wall coverings and matching light pastel fabrics are used throughout. Country armoires, house televisions, and plush robes hang in the closets. Original art work, including many performing arts themes, grace the hotel walls.

Inn at the Opera provides excellent, personalized service. Morning newspaper, evening turndown, fine bath toiletries and wake-up calls are just a few of the standard services. The staff attends to personal and business needs, providing meeting rooms and secretarial service, tour and limousine arrangements. They will also obtain tickets to performing arts programs for you.

Act IV

Act IV, on the hotel's ground floor, offers gourmet dining. The Act IV lounge is a recognized meeting place for performing artists and patrons, political and civic leaders, and, of course, hotel guests. Rich wood and tapestry walls, thick carpeting and green leathered chairs offer a handsome, intimate setting. While a musician entertains nightly on the grand piano, guests sit by the fire and enjoy a pre- or post-theater drink. The lounge stocks the finest liqueurs available, including a collection of vintage brandies.

Entrées at the Act IV dining room, headed by French chef Christian Janselme, range from medallions of lamb with sherry, garlic and pine nuts to breast of duck in creamy green peppercorn sauce.

In the Center

Inn at the Opera is within easy walking distance of many of San Francisco's attractions. City Hall, considered one of the most beautiful public buildings in the United States, is just one block away. It is a magnificent 1914 structure housing municipal offices, civil and criminal courts that is well worth seeing. Across the plaza is the Public Library, built in 1916, shelving some 1.5 million volumes and several special collections. The 1913 Civic Auditorium, scene of conventions, sports and cultural events, occupies the plaza's south end.

To the west of City Hall is the San Francisco Museum of Modern Art. The permanent collection of 20th century art rotates on a regular basis and includes such masters as Matisse, Klee and Picasso.

The Performing Arts

Inn at the Opera is across the street from the 3,535 seat Opera House. Built in 1932, it is home stage to the San Francisco Opera and the Ballet.

Louise M. Davies Symphony Hall is the lavish home of the San Francisco Symphony. The 1980 built hall greatly increased the city's cultural capacity, permitting longer seasons for the performing arts.

Downtown Shopping

Ten blocks east of the Inn at the Opera is Union Square, hub of San Francisco's downtown, where elegant stores cater to uptown tastes and fashions. The cable car runs from Union Square up Powell Street to Chinatown to the east or Nob Hill to the west. Chinatown is one of the largest Chinese communities this side of Asia, and hops day and night with activity. Nob Hill is the posh crest of the city from which has spectacular views of the entire bay area. There are several high-rise hotels with rooftop lounges for a 360 degreee view.

The popular Act IV Lounge is on the ground floor.

From Union Square, it is an interesting walk down Post Street to the Financial District. En route to the Financial District along Post, one passes the Crocker Galleria, a shopping arcade canopied by a glass vault 70 feet high and 275 feet long. The Financial District is bounded by Kearny Street to the west, Washington Street to the north and Market Street to the southeast. The most distinctive building in the area is the Transamerica Pyramid, which reaches 853 feet into the sky. The Bank of America, which houses its world headquarters here, is a close second at 778 feet.

Getting There

From the south take Highway 101 north. Exit on Fell/Laguna. Take Laguna to Fulton and turn right. From the north, take Highway 101 south toward Van Ness/Civic Center. Turn right on MacAllister, left on Gough and then left again on Fulton. The hotel is on Fulton between Franklin and Gough.

SPENCER HOUSE

Address:	1080 Haight Street, San Francisco, CA 94117
Telephone:	(415) 626-9205
Hosts:	Jack and Barbara Chambers
Room Rates:	$95 to $155 double. Includes full European breakfast.
Credit Cards:	For reservation guarantee only
Remarks:	Children over 12 welcome. No pets. No smoking in rooms.

There is nothing more delicious than the taste of discovery. The possibility of uncovering a treasure can take us on many an unmarked road, up many an unfamiliar step. One such step leads to a Victorian residence that has no posted name other than "1080." The travelers who discover San Francisco's Spencer House have indeed uncovered a treasure.

Love Through The Ages

The Victorian grandeur of The Spencer House, which stands on three city lots, commands attention from all who pass by this unpretentious corner of Haight Street. The tunnels of 1960's love and euphoria have changed considerably the last 20 years, although few people willingly relinquish their love-in memories (a misconception that's just fine with the residents of the area).

And though the follies of youth have been traded for maturity and experience, the Haight of the 1990's has no need to call attention to itself. It is simply a quiet, safe neighborhood where people who remember each other's birthdays still celebrate each other's successes.

Once Again

"We wouldn't live anywhere else in the world," says Barbara Chambers of the 8,000-square-foot mansion she shares with her husband Jack. Long time residents of San Francisco, the Chambers have capitalized on a tendency towards wanderlust through Jack's career as an airline pilot. With a love for the Bordeaux and Burgundy regions of France, Jack and Barbara started a successful wine import/distributorship based in the City. So the Chambers weren't particularly in the market for buying another home – until they took a quick peek at the Spencer House. The image wouldn't fade away. "You could feel it shudder under the weight of disgrace," recalls Barbara. And so, with a desire to erase the years of abuse and replace them with elegance and dignity, the Chambers purchased the Spencer House in 1984.

They retrieved old drawings and information about its past, specifically its late-19th century owner, John C. Spencer, who, with his wife and five children, made the house so self-sufficient that they used the spacious attic as a tennis and basketball court.

New ideas were integrated with old, and artistic neighbors offered their expensive services for free – the salvation of a once noble house was a cause worthy of donation.

The house's original Lincresta Walton wainscoting and intricate oak paneling again took on a lustrous sheen, and its magnificent chandeliers need only tender loving care to sparkle with radiance. Walls were covered with fabrics brought over from London, ceilings were molded, floors were polished, handsome oriental rugs added to accent four poster antique beds. Each of the mansion's six rooms has a double, queen or king size bed, its own private bath of marble and hand laid tile and a distinctive warmth and elegance.

The Chambers' Spencer House is truly their home. They are living in the spacious area on the top floor where the courts used to be. Their telephone number is unlisted and there is no sign out front announcing their existence. To anyone who passes by the house nothing more than a beautiful private residence. This is exactly how the Chambers like it and exactly how you'll feel while visiting – as a personal guest of the family who shares their world and their enjoyment of life.

Nights in White Linen

After a night spent in soft white linens and featherbed comfort, you'll enjoy a breakfast that is an experience truly to be savored. Fine china and silver accessories are laid out in a richly ornamental dining room. Barbara's fruits and berries are served in a light Chambord or Framboise syrup, followed by perfectly poached eggs Benedict with a homemade hollandaise, tiny corn and date nut muffins, fresh squeezed juice and hot coffee.

Better Than Being At Home

The bedrooms are all on the second floor, leaving the entire first floor for guest use. The floors, where hippies used to roller skate and now restored and polished. The large living room and sitting rooms are so comfortable you may be tempted to join Barbara in kicking off your shoes and padding around barefoot. The kitchen becomes the gathering place, just like at home. Fresh coffee is always on and the opportunity for conversation is always available.

The City by The Bay

San Francisco, as we all know, is a sensory extravaganza, but Barbara can help newcomers sort out the possibilities. The Haight's central location lets you

The linen-covered padded walls create quiet rooms.

be at the shopping meccas of Union Square or Union Street in minutes. Cable cars provide access to the Wharf and The Cannery. There are dozens of museums, changing exhibits at the Palace of Fine Arts and numerous cultural events throughout town. You can don roller skates in scenic Golden Gate Park, fly a kite at the Marina Greens, spend the day at the zoo, sail under Golden Gate Bridge or take the ferry to Alcatraz or Sausalito.

The City boasts the best of culinary achievement, offering restaurants whose chefs are internationally acclaimed. And you can top the day off with an after dinner liqueur, drinking in breathtaking views from the top floor of the BankAmerica building's posh Carnelian Room. At the end of the day, there's nothing better than returning to The Spencer House.

Getting There

Take Highway 101 toward the Golden Gate Bridge to the Laguna-Fell Street exit. Stay on Fell Street and travel approximately 10 blocks to Baker Street. Turn left on Baker Street until it dead-ends at Haight Street. Spencer House sits on the left corner of Haight and Baker.

THE MANSION AT LAKEWOOD

Address: 1056 Hacienda Drive, Walnut Creek, CA 94598
Telephone: (415) 946-9075
Hosts: Mike and Sharyn McCoy, Owners
                 Alice Johnson, Innkeeper
Room Rates: $125 to $200 double. Includes continental
                 breakfast.
Credit Cards: MasterCard, Visa
Remarks: Children over 13 welcome. No pets. No smoking.

Can a journey into a world behind white wrought iron gates bring time to a standstill? Can life there produce "happily ever afters" with the blink of an eye? Perhaps it has something to do with the White Rabbit that darts past, muttering that his Timex, has again, stopped ticking. In any case, guests, after only a few days amid the pleasures of The Mansion at Lakewood, are only too happy to give credence to chivalry, true love and, of course, white rabbits.

Rebirth of a Victorian Country Manor

In appropriate wonderland fashion, The Mansion at Lakewood has quite a story to tell. Originally part of a 2,000 acre Mexican land grant to the Pacheco family in 1834, the land was purchased by an early Walnut Creek settler in 1855. In 1908, the developer of the now beautiful Lakewood area, Robert Nobel Burgess, bought the property and, by adding expensive embellishments, transformed a farmhouse into a country manor for entertaining businessmen and friends in luxurious style. But as the city and its masses spread closer to the countryside, the days of afternoon croquet and high tea were no longer in style. And the estate, progressively surrounded by suburbia, faded into disrepair.

Mike and Sharyn McCoy, twelve-year residents of Walnut Creek, were able to rescue the remaining three acre parcel from the grips of a subdivision, but not without a fight. For more than a year, permits and public hearings kept the McCoys' hands tied. And it wasn't until Christmas 1988, after a full year of careful and costly renovation, that the restored Victorian masterpiece was opened to the public.

Through a 19th-Century Looking Glass

In a suburban city full of the impatience of the young, The Mansion at Lakewood clings to the elegance and dignity of a bygone era, paying the 20th century little mind. Beyond The Mansion's gates lies a protective haven, one that provides solace to all who enter.

After ringing the original hand crank doorbell (stamped October 23, 1860) and stepping through, you'll be struck by the whimsy of the assorted inanimate rabbits that peek at you from inauspicious places. Mike's playful humor and Cheshire cat grin belie his career as a nuclear engineer. And Sharyn's twinkly-eyed introduction to an innkeeper named Alice – who will present you with freshly baked cookies and homemade lemonade – well, it's enough to make you think that you may be in Wonderland after all.

The manor's seven handsomely appointed guest rooms – all with private baths and a distinctive appeal – are the product of Sharyn's and Alice's imagination and creativity. The attic Hideaway is tucked up against the stars, among piles of pillows and cozy nooks. The Summerhouse treats you to a canopied featherbed, atrium bath, sunny porch and private entrance. The coveted Estate Suite is a cloud of damask and soft goose down in an extraordinary raised platform antique brass bed with crackling fireplace, French doors that open onto a private terrace, and a gleaming black marble bath fit for royalty.

You will notice many thoughtful touches throughout the house – fresh cut wildflowers, turned down bed service with chocolates and orchids, and the opportunity to indulge in The Mansion's luscious continental breakfast at your leisure.

The Mansion's sunlight-filled drawing room, parlor and majestic library, which has a glowing marble fireplace, can be reserved for small corporate retreats or an intimate social gathering. Sharyn and Alice offer several house specialties including an Engagement Package complete with limousine service, a private suite and a candlelight dinner for two. The Mansion's expansive ground and gardens provide the perfect site for a romantic, old-fashioned wedding. Century old oaks, magnolias, eucalyptus and redwoods accent an assortment of wildflowers, cactus and the property's crown jewel: a vintage "smoke" tree, whose exotic woolly blossoms offer a special beauty.

And should you, in the midst of your discoveries, look up to find a respectable looking rabbit hiding beside the baseboards or under your bed, don't be alarmed. They, too, feel the magic of The Mansion.

The Hub of Bay Area Life

Walnut Creek has become one of San Francisco's preeminent bedroom communities. Only twenty-five miles from the heart of the city, The Mansion provides guests with easy access to a host of Bay Area activities and the added luxury of peace and quiet at the end of an energetic day. The Regional Center for the Arts has produced such an outstanding selection of plays, music, symphonies and cultural events that the United States Conference of Mayors declared Walnut Creek the most livable city for its size in the nation. Add to

Enjoy the seclusion of this Eastbay estate.

that the John Muir Museum, the annual Walnut Festival, the hiking, horse-back and water sports at nearby Mt. Diablo State Park and Lafayette Reservoir, and you'll agree that The Mansion at Lakewood provides the perfect location for whatever you want to do, wherever you want to go.

Getting There

From San Francisco, cross the Bay Bridge and take Highway 24 toward Walnut Creek to the Ygnacio Valley Road exit. Follow Ygnacio Valley Road approximately one mile to Homestead. Turn right on Homestead past one stop sign. The next left is Hacienda. Turn left on Hacienda to the white wrought iron entry gates of The Mansion.

THE WINE COUNTRY INN

Address:	1152 Lodi Lane, Saint Helena, CA 94574
Telephone:	(707) 963-7077
Hosts:	Jim Smith, Innkeeper and Sheila Ticen, Manager
Room Rates:	$111 to $133 double, $15 for additional person. Rates include Continental breakfast.
Credit Cards:	MasterCard, Visa
Remarks:	No pets. No children under 12.

The Wine Country Inn rests amidst the cultivated vineyards of Napa Valley, a part of California's famous wine producing region. Just as fine vintage wines are wrought of toil, dedication and love, so is this charming country inn.

Family Ties

One of the oldest continually operated inns in the region, The Wine Country Inn began as Ned and Marge Smith's dream. Intent on opening an inn, they traveled extensively on the East Coast to gather ideas. They wanted to recreate the look and character of older inns, yet combine it with the comforts available today. The Smiths engaged the entire family in the creation of their inn — the men to carry out the masonry, building and furniture refinishing, the women to stitch quilts, comforters and pillow slips. The result of their efforts was a three story stone and wood structure which, although completed only a dozen years ago, blends beautifully with the vintage wineries it neighbors.

Country Views

Because of the inn's placement on a knoll, almost every room offers a country view. Wild mustard, lupines and poppies flourish, and a row of Chinese pistachios line the driveway. Each of The Wine Country Inn's 25 rooms has a slight character trait which sets it apart from the others. Private balconies, large patios edging the lawn, snug window alcoves, a hand painted canopy bed, or a Victorian headboard reworked to handle a queen-size mattress all await your discovery. Fifteen of the rooms have a free-standing fireplace. All rooms have a private bathroom, air conditioning, and some have piped in classical music with individual volume control. The antique furnishings are from various periods; each has been hand selected by the Smiths.

Quiet Nooks

What each of the rooms has in common is comfort. There are no televisions or radios, yet there are plenty of books and quiet reading nooks. There are pastoral views and intimate rooms ideal for romance.

The inn has an outdoor swimming pool with plenty of lounge chairs around it, and a large bubbling spa nearby. Pool towels and robes are provided.

Hearty Continental Breakfast

The inn's Common Room is the gathering place for a hearty Continental breakfast served daily from 7:30 to 9:30 a.m. Homemade granola, a variety of breads from zucchini to banana, fresh juice, fruits and coffee comprise the morning meal. Guests can eat around the large refectory table or on the deck. The Common Room is also well stocked with books and games to keep you entertained during other times of the day. Pots of tea water and coffee steam continually. A refrigerator is also available for guests' use.

The Wine Country Inn is not far from over a dozen fine restaurants that serve lunch and dinner. Their menus are stacked on a Common Room table for guests to review, and the staff will be glad to make the phone call to secure a reservation. Now that's hospitality.

The Wine Country

Napa Valley is the largest and most popular of the wine regions in the state. Between the cities of Napa and Calistoga, over 210 wineries dot the valley. Their volume ranges from 500 case cottage wineries to million case producers. The valley evokes a somewhat European air with its miles of vineyards, small farmhouses and great stone wineries. Among the valley's old and great wineries are Beringer, Christian Brothers and Charles Krug. Spring Mountain Vineyard's Miravelle Mansion is noted for its role in the popular television drama *Falcon Crest.* Sterling Vineyards, which is accessible by tram, sits like a monastery on a knoll over the upper valley.

Most wineries in the valley are open to the public and offer tours and tasting, but a few wineries may be visited by appointment only. The Wine Country Inn staff will provide information on wineries and wine tasting and make appointments for guests as requested.

St. Helena, the wine country's capital, is noted for its 40 wineries and historic buildings. Chic shops, unique restaurants and scenic parks line the main street through town. The Silverado Museum features Robert Louis Stevenson memorabilia, where over 7,000 items recount his life and global adventures.

Enjoy the privacy of breakfast in bed.

Yountville, south of St. Helena, is noted for its historic, renovated brick and stone buildings. Vintage 1870 is a maze of small shops and eateries.

Calistoga, Yountville and St. Helena are artist communities, where galleries are filled with local paintings, crafts and photographs.

One of the best ways to view the wine country is via an early morning hot air balloon ride. Bicycling is popular in the valley, and hiking is enjoyed in the surrounding hills.

Getting There

From San Francisco, take the Oakland Bay Bridge to Highway 80, then head northward to the Napa cutoff. Travel Highway 29 through St. Helena, continuing one and three-quarter miles to Lodi Lane. Head east one-quarter mile to the inn, which will be on your left.

NAPA VALLEY BALLONS, INC.

Address: P.O. Box 2860, Yountville, CA 94599
Telephone: (800) 253-2224 toll free in California,
or (707) 253-2224
Rates: $155 per person
Credit Cards: American Express, Discover, MasterCard, Visa
Remarks: Reservations required.

Napa Valley is a valley for all seasons. Corridors of mustard plants radiate vibrant golden hues in spring, brilliantly lit against the dark wild oaks. Summer's fields are a quilt of earthy wheat browns and grapevine greens. In autumn, the vine's leaves are transformed into a patchwork of colors as rich as the grapes they bear. Amidst the groves of eucalyptus and pine, between the stands of ancient oaks, rest grand chateau wineries.

There are few better ways to experience Napa Valley than via a hot air balloon. The 26-mile long valley is known for its gentle, predictable winds, and most days are ideal for flying. Napa Valley Balloon, Inc. is well equipped to create a safe and memorable flying experience.

Established in 1978 with the launching of a single balloon, the company has expanded their fleet to fourteen. Eight pilots and a large supportive ground crew comprise the competent staff. Operated by four co-owners, it is the largest company in the valley, carrying about 8,000 passengers annually.

Dawn over Napa Valley

The Napa Valley ballooning experience begins at dawn, before the sun's warmth causes the winds to kick up. Balloons are launched from various sites in the valley, but often they leave from the Domaine Chandon Winery. As the balloon's gaping mouth is shot with flame it begins to rise like a giant awakening from a nap. The wicker gondola is then boarded by six passengers and a pilot, and the colorful, inverted pear balloon lifts gently from the earth.

Climbing to around 1,000 feet, the balloons ride the air currents, gracefully maneuvering through the valley. The elevation is altered by the degree of heat blasted into the balloon. The pilots scan the vista, assessing the winds, continually changing the balloon's altitude to steer by the currents.

When the balloon is ready to set down, 45 minutes to an hour after takeoff, a chase crew is waiting.

Champagne Celebration

Following the balloon flight, a champagne celebration takes place. A table spread with elaborate trays of cheeses, cold cuts, fresh bread, baskets of fruits, vegetables and dips, and pastries awaits. Champagne and orange juice flow freely as the successful flight is toasted. Napa Valley Balloons staff members join in the fun, snapping souvenir photos for participants, singing songs and ceremoniously presenting a balloon replica pin.

Ballooning is a safe sport, and the staff have a special knack for making the flight seem effortless and light hearted. They have flown with small babies and centenarians alike, and all land with a certain effervescent smile and a special memory of their lofty experience. No special clothing is required, except a hat for tall men. The only thing you really need to bring is a camera.

Always reconfirm your departure time and location the night before, although the final launch decision is not made until sunrise.

Getting There

Yountville is on Highway 29 north from Napa. Directions to the specific meeting spot will be given upon confirmation of your reservation.

Experience the wine country in a special way.

THE FOOTHILL HOUSE

Address: 3037 Foothill Boulevard, Calistoga, CA 94515
Telephone: (707) 942-6933
Hosts: Susan and Michael Clow
Room Rates: $85 to $175 double. Includes a continental breakfast.
Credit Cards: MasterCard, Visa
Remarks: No pets. No smoking.

Samuel Brennan was a smart man. Not only did he predict, way back in 1850, that the Napa Valley's grape growing region would become an international destination, but he identified the herbal mud baths of Calistoga's hot mineral springs as a medicinal treatment of uncommon power.

Though the 20th century has seen Sam's forecast for modern day Calistoga come true, the Napa Valley city has miraculously maintained its Old West, Gold Rush days, small town atmosphere. It offers the perfect retreat from life's excesses and stresses, as well as the excitement of a Wine County tour.

Deceptive Appearances

Mike and Susan Clow first visited Calistoga on their honeymoon and ended up staying in a less than romantic mainstreet motel and left them none too eager to return. "We hated it," said Susan.

But Mike and Susan Clow are not your ordinary Midwestern high school sweethearts. Yes, they reflect the down to earth values of hard work, honesty and commitment. But they also had a dream and a prediction of their own. They shared a "clear as a bell" memory of a particularly elegant retreat they visited in Bayfield, Wisconsin – the Old Rittenhouse Inn. "This gracious couple presided over a most luxurious estate, with servant and staff at their beck and call, and played host to those who could indulge in such refined living. "Every day," Susan explained, they served tea in the parlor. And they had this handsome little son who played quietly under a gorgeous grand piano. I wanted a life like that."

So with remarkable patience, the Clows, living in Chicago, started researching, asking questions, looking at property. Susan took up quilting and started buying antiques. Michael pursued his interest in winemaking, anticipating the day when a place such as the Franz family farmhouse would appear on their horizon.

The Best of Beds

"I have to laugh at myself now," chuckles Susan, whose six year old daughter Alexi couldn't stay still under a piano for five minutes. And the Clows' newest addition, Eric, is a toddler in constant motion. So, although the Clows' daily life at Foothill hasn't the ease or leisure of their original dream, it is indeed rich in healthy, happy family environment which the Clows share with their guests. Mike and Susan's warm, personal style of hospitality have made Foothill House one of the *Frommers Guide's* 100 best bed and breakfast homes in North America.

Mike and Susan remodeled their simple turn of the century house into suite-sized guest rooms, each with its own private entrance and queen-sized four poster bed covered with one of Susan's handmade quilts. Country antiques are accented with woodburning fireplaces for chilly winter evenings, air conditioning and ceiling fans for the summer months, a stereo cassette player with a selection of music, complimentary wine and Calistoga water and a private bath with handmilled soaps. Turn down service each evening includes a decanter of fine sherry and a tiny jar of Susan's homemade "Sweet Dream" chocolate chip cookies.

The Evergreen Suite, described as one of the Wine Country's most romantic, pampers you with a whirlpool jacuzzi tub, cozy day bed, a private library and its own private garden deck view of Mt. St. Helena. The free standing Quail's Roost, now being remodeled, will offer all the amenities of the perfect lover's retreat. "It will be fun to offer our guests the kind of honeymoon we wish we had!" said Susan.

As Well as Breakfast, Etc.

Morning is a particularly pleasant time in the Sun Room at Foothill House. Your first cup of freshly roasted coffee is followed by one or another of Susan's tasty homemade breads and muffins, accompanied by fresh fruits and juices, coffee and teas. You can have breakfast delivered to your room or out on the terrace, where the early morning view displays the beauty of the valley.

In every detail, Mike and Susan go out of their way to make you feel at home. They will be in the driveway to greet you as you arrive. You become part of the family as Alexi takes your hand and leads you out onto the terrace for "wine appreciation hour." Mike will let you in on some of the valley's best kept secrets, while Susan helps you plan your stay, from winery tours to restaurants and everything in between.

Napa Valley From its North Side

The beauty of Foothill House's Calistoga location is that it affords all the conveniences of the Napa Valley without the headaches and frustrations of the

The Evergreen suite has all the comforts for a romantic time.

traffic and the crowds that gather further south in the valley. The Sharpsteen Museum in downtown Calistoga has fine shops and galleries, and the town has its own sailplane center. Calistoga's bubbling mud baths begin with a soak in warm volcanic ash, peat moss and mineral water, followed by a mineral water bath, sauna, blanket wrap and massage.

Go ahead and indulge in the sweet fragrance and heady sips of the Napa Valley's champagnes and wines. With more than 210 wineries to choose from, you can taste your way from one end of the valley to the other. The miles and miles of tended vineyards bring a taste of Europe to California and offer spectacular scenery every season of the year.

Getting There

Take Highway 29 north into Calistoga, where the road intersects Highway 128 and becomes Foothill Boulevard. Follow Foothill Boulevard one and one-half miles past Lincoln Avenue. The Foothill House's small sign will be on the right and the driveway on the left.

TOLL HOUSE

Address:	15301 Highway 253, P.O. Box 268, Boonville, CA 95415
Telephone:	(707) 895-3630
Host:	Beverly Nesbitt, Owner and Innkeeper
Room Rates:	$60 to $100 double; additional person $15, includes country breakfast
Credit Cards:	Personal and travelers checks preferred. MasterCard and Visa accepted.
Remarks:	No young children or pets.

(stamp overlaid: UNDER NEW MANAGEMENT — HAS NOT BEEN REINSPECTED)

The Toll House country inn sits quietly nestled in the firs of Bell Valley. In the heart of Mendocino County, it is just minutes from internationally recognized wineries, and less than an hour from the magnificent Mendocino Coast. The Toll House is small, lending it a cozy, friendly appeal.

Built in 1912, The Toll House was once headquarters for the Miller Family Ranch, a sheep grazing and hop growing holding. An intermediate owner had begun renovation with the thought of creating a hunting lodge. Former model and seafarer Beverly Nesbitt purchased the property in 1981. "I was walking two feet off the ground the first time I saw the house," she says. "Each room was better than the previous one."

The Captain's Return

Beverly learned that Highway 253, which runs in front of the inn, was once a toll road for tree haulers. Thus it seemed only appropriate to name her inn the Toll House. She redecorated the house with a theme reminiscent of her ocean-going days. "I call it the Sea Captain's Return," Beverly says. "It's the type of place a sea captain would wish to come home to."

The Toll House has five guest rooms, each very distinct. The Library, beautifully appointed in rich greens and burgundy, is oriented for wheel chair access. It is the largest room, featuring a fireplace, private bath, sun porch and a queen-size Murphy bed. A ship's brass nameplate hangs above the fireplace. The Blue Room is tastefully decoated, and has a fireplace and private bath, too. Mollie's and Kathy's rooms, named for one of Beverly's daughters and a granddaughter, are very spacious and share a bath. Mollie's rose, black, blue and rust colors are beautifully coordinated in the wallpaper and fabrics. Kathy's room is a cheery blend of peach and lime. Both contain a queen and twin bed. The Bicycle Shed is a small, barnlike building just behind the main house with two twin brass beds cozily made with plaid flannel linens and scarlet spreads. The bathroom is across the courtyard in the main house.

Tiered wood decks lead from the house to the gardens. A hammock swings lazily under a tree, where guests can lounge with an engaging novel. An inviting hot tub whirls in a nearby wood gazebo.

Beverly pays special attention to guests' comfort by doing such things as providing a bottle of chilled local wine for them upon arrival and furnishing each room with a diary-like book for guests to share thoughts and stories. These notes are fun to read before snuggling between sheets already warmed by a sheet warmer.

Country Feast

Beverly is an accomplished cook who takes great pride in her hearty country breakfasts. In the pleasant, airy dining room overlooking the gardens, guests dine on one of the daily Toll House specialties: Belgian waffles topped with pure maple syrup, New Zealand bacon and egg pie, and freshly baked breads. Fresh fruits, juice and fresh ground coffee accompany the meal.

Dinner at the inn, a fixed price, multi-course feast prepared and elegantly presented by Beverly, may be arranged with advance reservations. One of the more popular entrées is "Margaret Parducci's Lamb," from the well-known local winery owners' ranch. Guests are welcome to bring their own wine and liquor for the evenings meal.

There are a number of restaurants in nearby Boonville, Mendocino and Ukiah. Beverly will gladly assist in making an appropriate selection.

Central Location

The Toll House is in close proximity to a diversity of activities. Mendocino County is a noted wine producing region, with several major wineries within easy driving distance. The Parducci family, who have been making wine in the area for three generations, will take you on an interesting tour.

Boonville

The small town of Boonville, just four miles from the Toll House, is known for "Bootling," a dialect derived from English, Scotch-Irish and Indian words. It is said that the language was created by the younger generation to confuse adults and outsiders. Many local signs capitalize on its uniqueness, and some residents are fluent.

Anderson Valley extends from Boonville to the town of Navarro, spanning some of California's most dramatic scenery. It is an area of excellent wines, and many small wineries here are gaining recognition. A drive on Highway 128 is a pleasurable way to spend the day. Bird watching, picnicking, hiking and photographing should be on the agenda along the Navarro River.

Private dinners can be arranged.

The Pacific Coast, with its vintage town Mendocino, is less than an hour from the Toll House. An exceptional array of shops and galleries, as well as fine restaurants and a repertory theater, await in this delightful town. One mile north of town, Russian Gulch State Park is laced with hiking and biking trails through dramatic fern canyons.

Back at the Toll House, Beverly's dogs Raley and No-Name sit quietly on the front porch. Adjacent to the property, over 1,200 acres of private land, to which guests have access, await exploration.

Getting There

Heading north from San Francisco, take Highway 101 to Ukiah, then Highway 253 (Boonville Road) west for eleven miles. From the coast, take Highway 128 to Boonville then Highway 253 east about six miles.

WHALE WATCH INN
BY THE SEA

Address:	35100 Highway 1, Gualala, CA 95445
Telephone:	(707) 884-3667
Hosts:	Irene and Enoch Stewart, Owners
Room Rates:	$135 to $210 double. Two-night minimum on weekends. Three-night minimum on holiday weekends.
Credit Cards:	American Express, MasterCard, Visa
Remarks:	Rates include breakfast. Not suitable for children. No pets. Smoking on decks only.

Perched on the western edge of the continent, 100 steps above Anchor Bay on the Mendocino Coast, the Whale Watch Inn has been described as "a jewel of peace and tranquility," a "haven for lovers in love." The inn's 18 luxurious suites creatively enhance the romance and solitude of the property's spectacular ocean views. Pampered by a warm and gracious staff dedicated to preserving a guest's privacy, an experience at the Whale Watch Inn is indeed the ultimate revenge for a harried and hectic world.

The inn began nearly two decades ago when Irene and Enoch Stewart were drawn to the northern California coast to seek refuge from a busy city life. They were enchanted by the scenic beauty and the "banana belt" climate that also offered a perfect lookout for spotting migrating whales. Ten years after building their second home on the cliffside acreage, the Stewarts decided to share the rejuvenating powers of their retreat with others. The inn is now comprised of five separate buildings.

Suite Selection

A feeling of serenity and harmony is instilled through the Stewart's attention to detail. Soft shades of pastels and vaulted ceilings with skylights enhance the mood of each room's interior. The queen-size beds are covered with lace-work linens and thick, down comforters. Fresh flowers, classical music and a cozy fireplace provide perfect ingredients for total relaxation. Private decks are ideally suited for sipping wine and watching the moonlight dance on the surf below.

Each of the 18 rooms has its own personality. The Silver Mist features a contemporary Art Deco motif and an elevated two-person whirlpool bath with a view of the fireplace and the ocean below. The Showcase Suite is elegantly

appointed with custom designed Queen Anne furnishings. Four suites in the Sea Bounty building offer fully equipped kitchens, making them ideal for longer stays. All rooms offer private entrances and decks, and are within walking distance to the beach.

The original Whale Watch building houses two small guest rooms and a library room that is dominated by a circular fireplace. Sofas, game tables and easy chairs make it the perfect place to curl up with a good book or reflect on the spectacular view. Wine and cheese are served around the fire on Saturday evenings. With no television or telephones, the atmosphere offers the utmost in peace and relaxation.

Breakfast in Bed

Breakfast is served in the individual rooms at pre-arranged times. The menu changes daily and may include cheese blintzes with wild blackberry sauce or mushroom-crusted quiche. Freshly-brewed coffee, juice, seasonal fruits, and homemade bread are always part of the fare.

If the day's adventures include a picnic on the beach or an evening by the fire, the Whale Watch staff will prepare a "snack basket" heaped with goodies, and complete with plates, silver and linens. The inn also offers a nice selection of imported and domestic wines and champagne.

Coastal Beauty

With no agendas and no demands, the Whale Watch offers plenty of opportunity to enjoy the surrounding beauty. A private stairway descends to the beach some 90 feet below the inn. Beach walking and tidepool exploring are year-round events. November through May is whale watching season. Tennis, golf and horseback riding are not far away, and six miles south of the Whale Watch along Highway 1 is Gualala Point Regional Area, where hiking trails ramble along bluffs and headlands. Beach access and picnic facilities are available.

The charming town of Gualala has a number of art, craft and photography galleries. This historic community has a colorful past: Pomo Indians, Russian trappers, Mexican land owners, German settlers and Chinese cooks have all had a hand in settling the area. A selection of restaurants is within a short drive of Gualala and the Whale Watch Inn. The inn staff is well acquainted with the area and happy to assist in making reservations.

Point Arena Lighthouse, approximately fifteen miles north of Gualala along Highway 1, stands on the point of the U.S. mainland closest to Hawaii. The area is site of countless shipwrecks. First constructed in 1870, the lighthouse stood until 1906 when the lens and tower were destroyed by the great San Francisco earthquake. The rebuilt tower has withstood the tests of time and

The Silver Mist Suite is a romantic hideaway.

the rigors of nature to this day. A museum at the base tells the story, and a tour includes a trip to the top.

Highway 128 runs eastward from the coast into the heart of the Anderson Valley and some of Mendocino's premium wineries. Between Philo and Navarro are a few of the smaller wineries, where visitors have a chance to sample wines and even meet the wine makers. The staff at the hotel will be happy to assist with arrangements.

Getting There

Take Highway 101 to Petaluma. Go west through Two Rock and Valley Ford to Bodega Bay. Follow Highway 1 north to the Whale Watch at Anchor Bay, five miles north of Gualala. Or, take Highway 101 to the River Road turnoff, four miles north of Santa Rosa. Go west through Guerneville to Jenner. Follow Highway 1 north to the Whale Watch Inn.

THE STANFORD INN
BY THE SEA

Address: P.O.Box 487, Mendocino, CA 95460

Telephone: (707) 937-5615

Location: At Coast Highway One and Comptche-Ukiah Road in Mendocino

Hosts: Joan and Jeff Stanford, Owners and Innkeepers

Room Rates: $115 to $190, including champagne breakfast

Credit Cards: American Express, Diners, Club, Discover, MasterCard, Visa

Remarks: Two-night minimum on weekends. Pets accepted.

The century-old town of Mendocino perches on a broad headland of Northern California's rugged coast. Once a thriving logging and ocean-going community, Mendocino's Victorian buildings are now home to art galleries, handicraft shops and fine boutiques. Mendocino's residents blend the polite reserve of their New England heritage with the casual, artistic flair of California coastal life. The result: an attractive town in a most spectacular setting. Mendocino is one of those rare travel finds that needs to be slowly savored. There are few better ways to appreciate the Mendocino area than by staying a few days at The Stanford Inn by the Sea.

The Stanford Inn by the Sea rides the shore of the Big River. Backed by a curtain of redwood forests, the inn faces the Pacific Ocean and overlooks Mendocino. Ancient apple trees from the historic China Gardens, lovingly cultivated rows of vegetables and flowers, and verdant lawns flank its hillsides. Ducks, swans and geese paddle around the pond while a family of llamas and a pair of robust Morgans graze nearby.

Joan and Jeff Stanford, former Carmel innkeepers, bought the property in 1980. At that time, a rather non-descript motel occupied the site. The Stanfords created a refined, comfortable country inn to take its place.

Country Charm

"What we wanted to create was a special experience," says Jeff Stanford. "That's why we built a true country inn where guests would feel at home." Each of the Inn's 25 rooms opens onto a deck, offering panoramic views of the ocean and the grounds. Each has private bathroom stocked with fragrant

soaps. Wood burning stoves and fireplaces add country fashioned warmth. The rooms are tastefully decorated with country floral prints, four poster queen- and king-size beds, authentic antiques and fine reproductions, and natural wood paneling. Plants and books create a homelike atmosphere, while a decanter of local wine on a silver platter adds a pampering touch. The Stanfords have a vast collection of local art which graces the rooms.

A small Nantucket style cottage near the river contains two lovely units equipped with full kitchen, separate bedrooms and a sitting room. A couple of miles down the road, the Larkin House accommodates larger groups in its three cozy bedrooms, living room and kitchen. It, too, offers an ocean view and all the Stanford amenities.

After a restful sleep, guests stroll into the cheery lobby to assemble their breakfast tray. Under a copper domed server are warm and delicious sweet rolls, especially designed for the lodge and baked in brick ovens. Juice, a basket of fruits, coffee or tea, yogurt, granola, hot cereals, melons and chilled champagne complete the meal. Guests may linger in the lobby, or may pick up the daily paper for a leisurely morning on their flower festooned deck. Either way, guests are guaranteed an unhurried start to the day.

Ever upgrading, the Stanfords plan to add ten deluxe suites adjacent to the main building, a dining room, and an enclosed swimming pool.

Catch-A-Canoe

The Big River winds through a forested canyon that opens into Mendocino Bay. Its undeveloped shores are home to a host of wildlife, including deer, black bear, beaver, blue heron and osprey. The first eight miles of the river are gentle tidal waters, ideal for swimming, canoeing and kayaking. The Inn owns and operates a canoe rental program called Catch-a-Canoe, and their fleet of nearly 40 canoes and kayaks are available for hourly or day-long excursions on this Class I river. After a brief lesson and a few pointers, you paddle can into the wilderness for exploration, photography, fun and relaxation.

Coastal Wanderings

The Northern California coast offers intriguing sights in any season. The windswept shore is often battered by winter storms, which bring in driftwood, shells and other treasures dredged from the sea. A long, beautiful beach is just minutes from the lodge, offering prime strolling, picnicking and sunbathing. Experienced scuba divers may explore the undersea world, while fishing enthusiasts reel in salmon and steelhead.

The Inn loans Cannondale mountain bikes, the fat-tired version of traditional bikes, for jaunts into Mendocino or along forested backroads. Logging roads lace the hills beyond the lodge where bikers ride among redwoods and firs.

All the bedrooms have a fireplace.

Fort Bragg lies along the coast to the north of Mendocino. As the terminus of the famous "Skunk" railroad, it is an attraction for families and railroad buffs. A round trip on the railroad, which takes about six hours, crosses 31 bridges and trestles as it meanders through the redwoods.

Strolling Mendocino's boardwalk, one discovers nearly 50 galleries and shops. Fine restaurants are found in the town and along the coast, and the staff at The Inn is very helpful in directing guests to the better finds. Van Damme State Park, also near the inn, has interesting pygmy forests, and Mendocino National Forest offers over one million acres of protected land.

Getting There

From Highway 1, head east on the Comptche-Ukiah Road just south of Mendocino. The inn is clearly marked on your left.

BENBOW INN

Address:	445 Lake Benbow Drive, Garberville, CA 95440
Telephone:	(707) 923-2124
Hosts:	Chuck and Patsy Watts
Room Rates:	$83 to $240 double. Off season and holiday rates available
Credit Cards:	American Express, MasterCard, Visa
Remarks:	Complimentary afternoon-tea and scones; hot mulled wine in spring and fall; hors d'oeuvres daily. Closed after Thanksgiving until mid-April, except over Christmas holidays.

The throngs of Northern California's mighty redwoods part just enough to make room for a privileged few: the highway, Eel River, and the Benbow Inn.

The 1926 English Tudor inn rests on the banks of the Eel River and, in summer when the river is backed up, Lake Benbow. It is an elegant, historic hotel once frequented by the likes of Herbert Hoover, Eleanor Roosevelt and Charles Loughton. Through a succession of five owners, the inn underwent many changes and various states of disrepair. Present owners Chuck and Patsy Watts purchased the Benbow in 1978 after owning and operating a successful Carmel inn. In the years that followed, they restored the Benbow Inn to its former state of grace and grandeur, adding their own sensibilities and tastes. If the measure of a fine inn is its degree of comfort, then the Benbow ranks among the best.

Riverside Inn

The Benbow is edged by the gentle Eel River and a well-maintained lawn. All of the rooms in the four story inn offer a view of the river, the redwoods or the grounds. All 55 rooms have a private bath, air conditioning and central heating. Original art graces the walls, and a basket of amenities and another of books are a few of the extras. A carafe of sherry awaits arriving guests, and a coffee maker sits ready to perk. The Terrace and Garden rooms border the river and sport terraces with white lawn furniture, color TV and VCR. Three rooms feature a wood burning fireplace, VCR and refrigerator; one has a jacuzzi and wet bar.

Guests arriving in the afternoon may likely be swept from one form of merriment to another. Tea and scones are the mid-day ritual; hot mulled wine is offered in spring and fall. Both are served in the spacious lobby, decorated with antiques and jazz era relics. A plush burgundy couch, when not occupied by Truffles, the fudge-colored Afghan, is the spot to pursue a good novel or

join others over a perplexing jigsaw puzzle. Glenn Miller music wafts from the juke box in the lounge, signaling it's time for hors d'oeuvres and a little cheer. The pub features a long mahogany bar and deep comfortable red leather love seats by the fire. This may be the only pub where you will ever find a life-size stuffed bear sitting casually at a window table, quietly sipping a martini and soaking in the casual atmosphere.

Adjacent to the pub is a small theater where films are shown nightly. The Watts have a collection of over 250 classic films, which they will also show during the day upon request.

Fine Dining

The Benbow Inn restaurant resembles one you'd expect to find in the English countryside. It is a romantic spot for a leisurely meal, and the chefs prepare the fresh California foods in innovative fashion. Breakfast, luncheon, Sunday brunch and dinner are available. Dinner reservations are recommended, especially during the peak summer visiting months. The à la carte entrées, which vary seasonally, may include duck with lingonberries and apple, rack of lamb with rosemary, or poached salmon with bay scallops, red wine and fresh herbs. An extensive wine list offers an ample selection of fine wines to accompany the meal.

Sunday brunch features a selection of entrées including eggs Benbow, a seafood version of the popular eggs Benedict, which also appears on the menu. French doors lead to a terrace off the dining room. The terrace overlooks the Eel River and is an enjoyable place from which to sample the fine cuisine and excellent service.

Special Events

Chuck and Patsy create a calendar to list their many special events.The Halloween Masquerade Ball is popular, as is the August Shakespeare in the Park. November is Wine Tasting, and December 31 is the annual Run for the Scones, in which guests run, walk or bike their way into the New Year. The inn is also an ideal spot for weddings or corporate gatherings.

Plenty to Do

The Benbow Inn is located near a host of activities, so guests never lack something to do. With Lake Benbow at the doorstep, swimming, kayaking, windsurfing, and paddling are a must. The state park rents canoes and rowboats. There are hikes around the lake, and the park department has installed a self-guided exercise trail. A 9-hole golf course is nearby, as are several tennis courts. Horseback riding, bicycle rentals, and hayrides can be arranged by the front desk staff.

Tea and scones are a mid-day ritual.

Visit the Giants

North of Garberville is a 33-mile scenic drive called the Avenue of the Giants. Following the South Fork of the Eel River, it winds through the Humboldt Redwoods State Park. Here, the tall redwoods are sometimes wide enough to drive through. In Scotia, a tidy community built entirely of redwood, is the Pacific Lumber Company mill. The largest redwood mill in the world, it offers an interesting visitor's center and self-guided tour.

Continuing north to Ferndale, visitors find a remarkable collection of Victorian homes. Picnic lunches are available for purchase from the dining room, and should be requested the night before.

Getting There

The inn is located two hundred miles north of San Francisco and about seventy miles south of Eureka. Off Highway 1, take the Benbow Exit and head west on Lake Benbow Drive. The inn is just ahead on the left.

THE GINGERBREAD MANSION

Address:	400 Berding Street, Ferndale, CA 95536
Telephone:	(707) 786-4000
Hosts:	Wendy Hatfield and Ken Torbert
Room Rates:	$75 to $110 double; suites $100 to $150. Rates include breakfast. Two-night minimum stay on weekends and holidays.
Credit Cards:	MasterCard, Visa
Remarks:	All rooms have private baths with showers. Smoking permitted on outside veranda only. No pets. Not suitable for children under 10.

Should the Yellow Brick Road have been surreptitiously diverted, it would surely have ended at the Gingerbread Mansion. A glowing beacon of warmth and hospitality, this unique bed and breakfast is set just off Ferndale's Main Street. The 19th century turreted structure portrays a fairytale world of enchantment and serenity.

The Cream City

The state historical landmark town of Ferndale, nestled in a quiet valley, is a wonderland of Victorian architecture. Nicknamed "Butterfat Palaces" by the Portuguese and Scandinavian dairymen who settled the area in the late 1800s, the ornate houses are still maintained by descendants of the "Cream City's" founding fathers. Ferndale is a perfect place to spend a weekend.

A blend of Queen Anne and Eastlake architecture with intricately detailed "gingerbreading", the Gingerbread Mansion was built in 1899 for a local physician, Dr. H. J. Ring. He turned it into the Ferndale General Hospital in the 1920s. In search of an alternative to their city lifestyles, Wendy Hatfield and Ken Torbert bought the mansion in 1981. With exhuberance, they created an elegant, romantic retreat.

"His and Her" Bubble Baths

Wendy and Ken's meticulous care is evident in every detail. All nine guest rooms are large and individually appointed with antiques, stained glass windows, period art pieces and comfortable, firm queen beds. Bathrobes are tucked in the dresser drawers.

Four rooms have wonderful old-fashioned, claw-footed bathtubs. Two of the suites boast a pair of these unique tubs. Complete with herbal bubbles, thoughtfully placed reading lamps, and walls adorned with a sampling of the Torbert's "bathing beauty" collectibles, these suites provide guests with a perfect balm for the overworked spirit.

Bountiful Breakfast

Enticing aromas lead guests into an elegant dining room for breakfast. The two tables are beautifully set with Ken's rare collection of green Depression glass. The dining room is gracefully adorned with glass embossed with tiny ballerinas and classic paintings of romanticized women. The Torberts play-fully refer to it as their room for "ladies in waiting."

A generous, European-style breakfast includes fresh fruits, juices, hard-boiled eggs, two kinds of locally made cheeses (salmon cheddar and caraway jack), and a variety of homemade breads, muffins and cakes. Wendy keeps your cup full with their special blend of Toddy coffee (just a hint of vanilla). Ken sprinkles the conversation with anecdotes from "Foggy Bottoms" history and its colorful cast of characters.

Many Extras

Four parlors offer opportunity to relax and enjoy. Two, with fireplaces, are stocked with an excellent collection of books and games. Afternoon tea is served in one of the parlors. The fourth invites guests to participate in the completion of one of two 1,000-piece jigsaw puzzles of the Mansion. No radios, TVs or telephones can be found in Ken and Wendy's optimally serene environment. (A parlor guest phone is available.)

For a more active visit, a fleet of one-speed bicycles (painted to match the house) is available. Galoshes and umbrellas make it possible to take a rainy day stroll around the garden—a magic wonderland of fountains, statuary and flowering plants. Early risers can always find a tray of coffee and juice on the hall sideboard. To close out the day, a turned-down bed with a hand-dipped chocolate on the bedside, set the stage for a night of sweet dreams.

Things to Do

Ferndale is a town of artisans and real people who take pride in their town. There is an abundance of curio shops, art galleries and museums; and often an antique show. The highly-acclaimed repertory theater hosts seven pro-ductions a year. The "Foggy Bottoms Milk Run" and the Bicycle Tour of the Unknown Coast" are two local sporting events. Memorial Day boasts the classic "World Champion Arcata-to-Ferndale Cross-Country Kinetic Sculp-ture Race"—a three-day affair where hundreds of entrants coax artistically welded piles of junk towards the finish line. In June, the Mid-Summer

The Fountain Suite has twin baths by the fire.

Scandinavian Festival takes over Main Street. At Christmas, Ferndale decorates America's tallest living Christmas tree—a 125-foot Sitka Spruce.

State and National redwood parks are north and south of town. Nearby Russ Park has miles of wilderness trails to explore. A long, untamed walking beach is but five miles from Main Street.

There is a very special driving loop from Ferndale out to the lost coast (the most unexplored region of the California Coastline). The loop continues over the mountains and comes back to Highway 101 through the redwoods.

Getting There

The Gingerbread Mansion is located two hundred sixty miles north of San Francisco, and about fifteen miles south of Eureka. Take the Fernbridge/ Ferndale exit off Highway 101. Follow the Ferndale-Victorian Village sign to Main Street (about five miles). Turn left on Brown Street. Go one block to Berding Street. The mansion is on the corner.

CARTER HOUSE AND HOTEL CARTER

Address:	Carter House – 1033 3rd Street, Eureka, CA 95501
	Hotel Carter – 301 L Street, Eureka, CA 95501
Telephone:	(707) 445-1390 (Carter House),
	(707) 444-8062 (Hotel Carter)
Host:	Mark and Christi Carter
Room Rates:	$75 to $165 double; includes full breakfast at Carter House or a Continental breakfast at Hotel Carter
Credit Cards:	American Express, MasterCard, Visa
Remarks:	Complimentary wine and hors d'oeuvres served from 6 to 7 p.m. in Carter House parlor and the lobby of Hotel Carter. No pets.

Mark Carter, a native Eurekan with a penchant for Samuel and Joseph C. Newsom designs (architects of the local Carson Mansion—recognized as the finest example of Victorian architecture in the United States), scratched an itch when he came across plans by the same architects for a smaller Victorian . The plans detailed the 1884 mansion that once stood in the middle of San Francisco until the great earthquake and fire of 1906. Carter House was inspired by some old Newsom drawings of the house that was destroyed in San Francisco's 1906 earthquake and fire.

It took Mark and a small crew sixteen months and $700,000 to build the Carter House. This truly romantic bed and breakfast inn opened in 1982 to immediate and rave reviews. The attention to detail in the big redwood home is impressive. The lavish detailing in the Carter House seven guest rooms is complemented by the simple interior design. Crisp white walls, polished oak floors spread with Oriental carpets, splashes of modern art—all add to the bright, uncluttered feel of the rooms. Cozy down comforters and flannel robes are part of the ambience. Four rooms have private baths. Three others share a light, spacious bath down the hall.

Guests staying at the Carter House have spread the news about the superb breakfasts. A typical morning might start with specially roasted coffee, freshly squeezed orange juice in a crystal glass, poached pear in caramel sauce, followed by a fruit muffin and a poached egg Benedict.

A New Challenge

Always ready for new challenges, Mark built Hotel Carter in 1986, to provide comfortable accommodations for Eureka's business travelers and those

seeking the benefits of a classic hotel. The Hotel Carter is a spacious twenty-room establishment which also houses an innovative restaurant. Reflecting the personality of its creator, it blends a contemporary California style with the old-fashioned values an Italian mother teaches her son—when strangers come to call, greet them with open arms, offer a warm fire, a glass of wine, and a houseful of laughter. Such is the hospitality you will find whenever you stay with Mark and Christi Carter.

The peach and ivory lobby of the Hotel Carter is enhanced by an eclectic display of contemporary art and bleached pine antiques. All rooms have private baths (some with Jacuzzis), telephones and televisions. Several rooms have fireplaces. The rooms come with a view of Old Town or the Marina, just a block away.

Experience in Dining

In "the smallest space you've ever seen" Christi Carter and her team of chefs produce innovative meals with style and creativity. "Everything is bought and prepared the same day," says Mark, "because we don't have space for a commercial freezer!"

The hotel offers a four-course dinner service three nights a week. With "fresh" as the key ingredient, the prix fixe menu features regional delicacies including North Coast seafood and a bounty of garden herbs and vegetables.

The dinner is worth any effort it takes to get to Eureka. The appetizer might be a salmon ravioli with saffron pasta in a lemon mustard cream sauce and tomato sauce. This is followed by a tarragon lavender sorbet. The entree may be a stuffed roasted filet mignon with a cabernet sauce, chiffonade of greens, scalloped potatoes, grilled garden peas and a trio of summer squash and tomatoes. Next, a course of gathered Maple Creek greens, wild herbs and flowers . Finally a chocolate hazlenut pate with chocolate sauce or meringue squares with lemon curd sauce, raspberries, currents and soft cream.

A Cultural and Recreational Cornucopia

The clean ocean air and smell of old traditions invites a tour through Eureka's Old Town. Explore the boutiques and antique shops or take a Victorian home tour. The Old Town area, once in a state of steady decline is now steadily improving and worth the time for an extensive walking tour. You are likely to find some of the sights associated with a working seaport as well as finding contemporary establishments. There are also three repertory theaters that offer year round performances. There are multitudes of festivals like the annual Rhododendron Festival, the Blackberry and Octoberfest Festivals which celebrate the area's ethnic and natural color.

Carter House has the comforts of an intimate home.

The grandeur of the North Coast wilderness is best illustrated by the Avenue of the Giants, just south of Eureka. The "Lost Coast" offers unlimited pristine beauty for those seeking solitude.

Humboldt Bay Cruises and the Arcata Marsh Sanctuary provide appreciation of the area'as diverse marine and wildlife. For a less isolated experience, the Skunk Train provides daily transportation between Willits and Fort Bragg, via the Emerald Forest.

Getting There

Take Highway 101 to Eureka. From the north, follow Highway 101 into town (it becomes 4th Street) to L Street. Turn right. Go one block. From the south, follow Highway 101 through town. It turns right onto 5th Street. Follow 5th Street thirteen blocks to L Street. Turn left. Go two blocks.

Pacific
Northwest

What Northwesterners know, they're not saying. They're not letting on that their region is one of the last unspoiled areas of the country.

Both Oregon and Washington are states made up of small towns. Portland and Seattle are the only cities of any size, the both states are dotted with hundreds of small towns. Many of them were once lumber towns. The mills employed just about everyone in town. Much of that is gone now and in its place are dozens of small tourism-related businesses are springing up, much to the delight of visitors.

If you search them out you will find old time country stores dating from the 19th century, antique shops, rural fishing villages and family vineyards. Perhaps the real find in the Northwest are the people.

There is a very strong pioneer streak in the people who call this region home. They tend to be very independent, to vote liberally and live conservatively. Never known as an easy place to live when compared to the more sunny climates, those who have come and stayed are fiercely loyal to this green and sometime soggy shoulder of the nation. Most couldn't imagine living any where else.

This love of area does not mean that Northwesteners are unfriendly or don't want visitors. On the contrary. The Northwest is full of some of the friendliest and most welcoming folks you'll find anywhere. What they do ask though is that you respect and treat their area as they do.

Wet Side and Dry Side

The Cascade Mountain Range splits the states in half from North to South. The Cascades extends some 750 miles from British Columbia into Northern California. Washington's Mount Rainier, reaching a height of 14,410 feet is the highest peak in the Cascades. Mount Hood in Oregon is a majestic cone shaped peak where skiing is available through the summer.

The Western side of the Cascades is the wet side due to the greater amount of liquid sunshine received. Seattle receives about 34 inches annually, Atlanta, New York and Chicago all get more. Nonetheless, the skies are often grey and it might drizzle at any time of the year.

The Eastern slope is much drier, warmer in the summer and colder in the Winter. This is primarily farming country and for the most part, flat.

Natural Playground

The Northwest is a region where people actively participate in the outdoors. The number of activities you can sample on a vacation is only limited by the amount of time you have to spend.

Pick one or two of the places featured in this book and plan to spend several days at each one. Have the innkeeper set you up with a local river rafter, naturalist, fishing charter or what ever is of interest to you. But do get out into the country and off the main roads.

Wineries

Oregon and Washington have a developing wine industry. For the past twenty years a variety of fine vinefera grapes have been planted. The different growing climates are creating wines that are acheiving international acclaim.

Within a 35-mile radius of Portland there are a number of excellent wineries available for tours. For more information contact the Oregon Winegrowers Association 1324 S.W. 21st Avenue, Portland, Oregon 97201.

In Washington the Yakima River Valley and the Columbia River Basin produce premium grapes. These regions exhibit many similarities to the great wine growing areas of France, in latitude and climate.

Liquor Laws

Legal drinking age in the region is 21. Liquor is sold by the bottle in state run liquor stores. The stores are not very visible or located for convenience. Since they close early and are not open on Sunday make your plans accordingly. Beer, wine and liquor are sold by the drink daily from 6 a.m. to 2 a.m. Driving while or after drinking is a very serious matter and strictly enforced.

Driving Laws

The speed limit is 65 mph on the rural highways and 55 mph in the urban areas. All people in the car must wear a seat belt. A right turn is permitted following a full stop at a red light. Radar is widely used, in the rural areas spotter planes are added to the arsenal.

Information Sources

Oregon Economic Development Department
Tourism Division
595 Cottage Street N.E.
Salem, Or 97310
(800) 547-7842 (out of state)
(800) 233-3306 (Within state)

Tourism Development Division
101 General Administration Building
Olympia, WA 98504
206) 586-2088

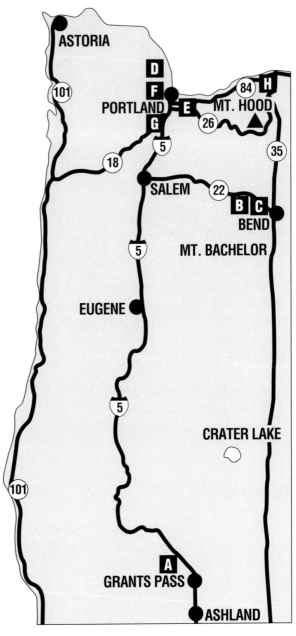

OREGON SPECIAL PLACES

A Paradise Ranch
B Black Butte Ranch
C Rock Springs Guest Ranch
D RiverPlace Alexis
E Genoa Restaurant
F Heron Haus
G Heathman Hotel
H Columbia Gorge Hotel

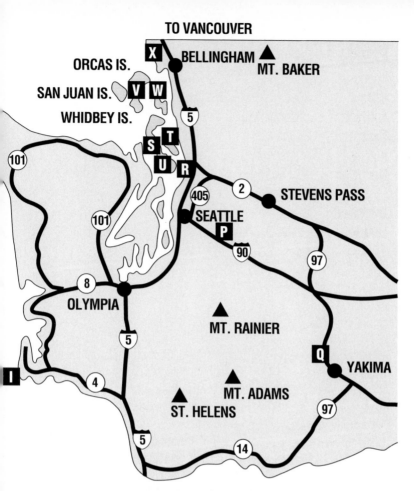

WASHINGTON SPECIAL PLACES

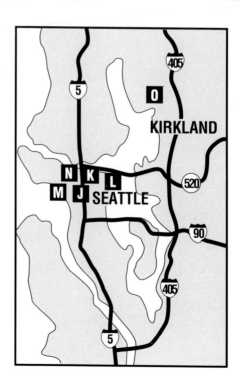

I Shelburne Inn and
  Shoalwater Restaurant
J Alexis Hotel
K Rover's Restaurant
L Dominique's Restaurant
M Inn at The Market
N Adriatica Restaurant
O Cafe Juanita
P The Herb Farm
Q Birchfield Manor
R brusseau's
S Home by The Sea
T Inn at Langley
U Saratoga Inn
V Turtleback Farm
W Christina's Restaurant
X Inn at Semiahoo

PARADISE RANCH INN

Address:	7000-D Monument Drive, Grants Pass, OR 97526
Telephone:	(503) 479-4333
Hosts:	Mattie and Ollie Raymond, Resident General Managers
Room Rates:	$69.50 to $96.50 single, $79.50 to $99.50 double. Additional person $20.
Credit Cards:	MasterCard, Visa
Remarks:	Honeymoon and winter packages available at special rates. Pets and children welcome.

The Rogue River carves a broad valley through southern Oregon, pausing in Grants Pass before making its final 50-mile journey to the Pacific Ocean. Sheltered by the coast and Siskiyou Mountains, the valley is graced with a moderate, dry climate year-round. Paradise Ranch Inn, on 310 acres in the valley floor, provides an excellent base from which to enjoy this scenic region. General managers Mattie and Ollie Raymond operate the inn with the assistance of family members. "We want guests to feel like they are a part of the family, like the ranch belongs to them," says Mattie.

Country Estate

Rimmed by a bright white fence, Paradise Ranch Inn resembles a gentleman's country estate. It was, in fact, a homestead cattle ranch when it was built in 1913. A white clapboard ranch house contains 18 guest rooms, six of which face onto a man-made pond. Country American decor prevails throughout. Rooms are furnished with queen- and king-size beds, and a spacious bathroom features a double-headed tiled shower. In keeping with the tranquil atmosphere of the inn, no televisions or phones are in the rooms. A phone is available in the nearby barn.

The House in the Woods is set apart from the inn, offering total seclusion for families or couples. Fully kitchen equipped, it sleeps up to eight in four bedrooms, each with king-size beds and private bath. A wood burning stove and hot tub are among the home's amenities.

The Barn is the gathering place for guests of all ages. The recreation center houses a grand piano, big screen television, pool and Ping-Pong tables, and a lounge area where guests can gather in front of the huge fireplace and enjoy a glass of wine before dinner.

Dining in Paradise

The Paradise Ranch Inn's dining room is beautifully set overlooking a tranquil pond. In the distance, the many layers of the Coast Range are highlighted by gentle mist and the setting sun. The dining room is presided over by one of Southern Oregon's finest chefs, who produces excellent cuisine based on seasonally available foods. Home grown vegetables and herbs are used, as well as only the freshest local meats and seafoods. Rack of lamb, scampi New Orleans, and Châteaubriand for Two are favorite dinner entrées. Chocolate-orange decaffinated coffee is the perfect accompaniment to the tempting array of desserts.

A hearty ranch breakfast and the Paradise continental breakfast get the day off to a fine start, and include homemade goods. Box lunches are available by request. A complete wine list features selections from Oregon as well as several imports.

Sense of Belonging

"What makes Paradise Ranch Inn special is that guests have a sense of belonging," says Mattie. "We have guests coming with their kids who came here as kids themselves."

Two lighted tennis courts on the grounds are utilized by guests for a nominal court fee. A tennis professional is available for private and group lessons as well as a stroke analysis video session. A ball machine may be rented on an hourly basis.

The swimming pool is the place to cool off after a game of tennis, and the hot tub swirls away those aches and pains. The ponds are stocked with trout and large mouth bass, and paddle boats are ready on the shore for an evening spin. A small island in the pond is equipped with a barbeque and a gazebo. It is an ideal spot for weddings and other special occasions. The inn has a fleet of mountain bikes available for guests' use, and maintains a couple of miles of trails for walking or riding. A three-hole triangular pitch-and-putt course provides family fun.

The latest addition to Paradise Ranch Inn will be an 18-hole golf course, targeted for completion in late 1990. With the completion of the course, additional guest rooms will be built.

Diverse Offerings

The Rogue River Valley offers a diversity of attractions, not the least of which is the Rogue River itself. Grants Pass is the headquarters for several licensed guides who offer fishing excursions on the river. One- to four-day trips are available on kayaks, rafts, drift boats and paddle boats. A two-hour jet boat

The restaurant overlooks ponds and the golfing area.

departs Grants Pass for 250-foot deep Hellgate Canyon. For landlubbers, a paved road winds along the Rogue northwest of Grants Pass, and hiking trails weave into the wild river section where no cars are allowed. Rogue fishing for sturgeon, steelhead and salmon peaks during winter, spring and fall.

The charming town of Ashland, nestled in the green foothills of the Siskiyous, is just south of Grants Pass along Interstate 5. Ashland is known for its excellent Shakespearean theater, the festival which lasts from late February through October.

Jacksonville, just 20 minutes from Ashland, conducts the Britt classical, bluegrass, jazz, dance and musical theater festivals from late June through September 1 in the beautiful Peter Britt gardens.

Getting There

From southbound I-5, take the Hugo Exit and turn right onto Monument Drive. Proceed four miles to the Paradise Ranch Inn, on your right. From northbound I-5, proceed to the Merlin Exit, north of Grants Pass. Turn left, then right onto Monument Drive. The inn is two miles down the road on the left.

BLACK BUTTE RANCH

Address:	P.O. Box 8000, Black Butte Ranch, OR 97759
Telephone:	(503) 595-6211, reservations (800) 452-7455
Location:	On U.S. Highway 20, eight miles west of Sisters
Host:	Wim Steenbakkers, President
Room Rates:	$50 standard room, $65 deluxe room, $95 to $145 one- to three-bedroom condo apartments, $90 to $155 two- to four-bedroom homes. Minimum stays during the summer season.
Credit Cards:	American Express, MasterCard, Visa
Remarks:	No pets, fireworks, motorcycles, scooters or off-road vehicles.

On the eastern slopes of Oregon's Cascade range, the ponderosa pine grow tall and stately, providing valuable habitat for deer, coyote, porcupine and raccoon. Eagles and osprey build their nests high in the pine's boughs, and squirrels, chipmunks and quail gather their seeds for food. At the 3,300-foot level, the pine give way to meadows and lakes, and it is here that Black Butte Ranch, Oregon's great golf and tennis resort, lies. Surrounded by seven Cascade peaks that range from the 6,415-foot cinder cone called Black Butte to the proud 10,495-foot Mount Jefferson, you might think that Black Butte Ranch would be dwarfed by comparison. Not at all. Sitting on the patios and decks of the ranch's condos and homes to watch the sun first light on the meadow, you would be hard-pressed to tell where the ranch ends and the Cascades begin.

Not a Carbon Copy

Black Butte Ranch is a destination resort unlike any other. Each unit in the 1,830-acre development is individually furnished and privately owned, but many are managed by the ranch rental program. The units have fully stocked kitchens (often including a dishwasher), washer, dryer, a rock or brick fireplace, television and telephone, wide inviting decks, housekeeping, and, most importantly, room to breathe. Guests receive the same privileges accorded the owners: full access to two golf courses, four swimming pools, 19 tennis courts, miles and miles of bike and jogging paths, and the lodge.

The lodge is the one building owned and operated by Black Butte Ranch. The three-story glass, fir and pine building is made all the more grand by the scale of the scenery outside its floor-to-ceiling windows. The furnishings combine

antique tables and secretaries with modern oak and fabric chairs. Accent rugs and tall potted plants cover the wooden floors. The rental accommodation desk and property sales office comprise the first level; the second houses the Lt. Henry Abbot and Elijah Sparks conference rooms, the restaurant and kitchen. On the uppermost floor, with an unrivaled view of the Cascades, is the lounge, where you can enjoy a full-service bar.

Conference facilities and a highly qualified staff who understand the importance of your meetings are available for small groups of up to 35 individuals at the Lodge.

Ranchmade Specialties

The restaurant, with its ringside seats overlooking Big Meadow and the cattle that graze there, is renowned in central Oregon for its regional cuisine. But the chef doesn't stop there. Ranch dinner specialties include generous cuts of prime rib, file of Petrole sole with tarragon butter, chicken scallopini, fresh Oregon steamer clams and New York steak. The wine list contains over 90 selections from Oregon, California, Washington and France.

Breakfast specialties include giant cinnamon rolls, ranchmade granola, eggs Benedict, and an omelette brimming with fresh ingredients. Lunch is an assortment of deli sandwiches, salads, a hot kettle of soup and fresh ranchmade bread, cheeses and fruit.

The Sporting Life

Golf is the main recreational activity at Black Butte Ranch, which was awarded a Silver medal by *Golf Magazine* as one of the top resorts in the country. Residents and guests play on two immaculately groomed 18-hole courses located amid the trees and within view of the mountains and lakes. Both the Big Meadow and Glaze Meadow courses are par 72 and are open seven days a week. The facilities include a driving range, practice greens and a pro shop. The ranch offers golf clinics throughout the summer, and golf pros are available to assist you with your game.

If golf has a rival at the ranch, that rival's name is tennis. There are 19 Plexi-Pave courts in seven different locations. In addition to special instruction classes for teens and adults, guests can arrange for private or semiprivate lessons. The ranch's sport shops rent rackets and ball machines.

Swimmers have no problem cooling off on Oregon's hot, dry summer days, for the ranch has four large pools and several wading pools for the little ones. Other activities include canoeing, or nearby horseback riding and whitewater rafting. There is fishing on the Deschutes and Metolius rivers or on the lake near the lodge. The ranch also offers 18 miles of paved biking trails. In addition, special golf packages are offered in the Spring and Fall.

The main lodge has meeting rooms, restaurant and lounge.

In the winter cross-country ski rentals are available at the Lodge Sport Shop. The lodge offers a special winter ski package.

Sisters, the small Western town eight miles east of the ranch, has only three streets, yet more than 70 businesses, shops and restaurants line them. Known as the llama capital of North America, the community has become a center for llama ranches. Should you choose not to leave the grounds, you can drive to the ranch's store for an amazing variety of foodstuff. The two sport shops sell books and magazines, clothing, and sporting equipment.

Getting There

U.S. Highway 97 is the main route through central Oregon. From the north, drive to Redmond, then turn onto Highway 126 and head for Sisters. From the south, drive to Bend, then take Highway 20 to Sisters. From the west, take Highway 22 from Salem, or Highway 126 from Eugene, which merges with Highway 20. The well-marked ranch turnoff is eight miles west of town.

ROCK SPRINGS GUEST RANCH

Address:	64201 Tyler Road, Bend, OR 97701
Telephone:	(503) 382-1957
Location:	Nine miles north of Bend
Host:	John Gill, General Manager
Room Rates:	$825 single, $1,495 double, per week, late June through Labor Day, American Plan; family rates are lower. Holiday rates from $85 per person, per day, modified American Plan.
Credit Cards:	American Express, Diners Club, MasterCard, Visa
Remarks:	No pets.

Nestled in the ponderosa pine and juniper tree country of central Oregon's Cascade foothills is Rock Springs Guest Ranch, a comfortable, unpretentious place where guests quickly get to know each other and become part of an extended family. It is a place with strong traditions and ties. In fact, over half of the guests return each year. At Rock Springs, guests usually gather in the lodge after dinner to play cards or chess, or just sit in front of the fire and chat.

Donna Gill, a lean, sinewy septuagenarian who was as comfortable splitting wood as she was riding a horse, is another tradition at the ranch — she's even a bit of a legend in this part of Oregon. Donna ran the ranch until she passed away less than a decade ago. She built the ranch with families in mind. Her nephew John now operates Rock Springs and continues the family tradition.

Catering to Families

Rock Springs Guest Ranch caters to families. Youngsters have their own counselors and programs to involve them in horseback riding, evening hayrides and lunch rides, organized talent shows, hikes, swimming and craft projects. And, while children are off exploring, adults have a chance to spend a little time together or join others at the cocktail hour. Families with children under five who require one-to-one supervision are invited to bring along their own babysitter. The ranch will provide sleeping accommodations and meals free of charge.

Eleven cozy, modern cabins are scattered among the tall ponderosa pines. Some have cathedral ceilings and knotty pine walls and accommodate six. Most have a fireplace; wood is stacked outside the door. Some cabins also have a kitchen, so you can prepare a snack or a full meal for yourself whenever you're hungry.

Rock Springs Guest Ranch operates on an American Plan from the end of June until early September. The week's package, which runs from Saturday to Saturday, includes all meals and activities. When winter comes, a modified American plan, which includes breakfast and dinner, is offered.

Nature's Song

In the early morning you wake to the songs of meadowlarks. The breeze through the trees sounds like distant surf. You're apt to see big gray, bushy-tailed squirrels, or bald and golden eagles that come to fish in the pond.

John Gill keeps about 55 horses for his guests, and great care is paid to the fitness of the riding stock. Whether a guest is a beginner or an eager, advanced rider, he or she can really enjoy the challenge and excitement of riding at Rock Springs. Once riders are assigned their horses, they are divided into small groups according to ability and set off on trails through the adjoining Deschutes National Forest, which is set against the backdrop of the magnificent snow-covered peaks of the Three Sisters.

Special Activities

For those who prefer not to ride, there is a swimming pool, lighted tennis courts, volleyball, horseshoes, croquet, fishing in the pond (stocked with bass and trout) and the option of doing nothing at all. The ranch also makes a good base for day trips to attractions in the Bend area. Among the favorites are Oregon High Desert Museum, Mount Bachelor for skiing (into July), Tumalo Falls, Pilot Butte State Park, fly fishing in top-rated Deschutes River, the spectacular scenery of Cove Palisades State Park, a day with the Indians on the Warm Springs Reservation and Lava Lands Visitors Center, Newberry Crater and the volcanic country south of Bend. There are also nine golf courses nearby.

At the end of the day, when activity slows and muscles grow tired, relax in the ranch's custom outdoor spa. Warm water spews from jets in the tiled bath set into a relaxing cave-like shelter of boulders. This is perhaps, the most romantic setting ever found for a hot tub.

Well-Fed Guests

Rock Springs Ranch feeds its guests well. Meals are served family style from the buffet. Breakfasts may include omelettes, homemade sticky buns, French toast, pancakes, waffles, fresh fruit and juices, ham, sausage or bacon and eggs. For lunch you can expect one hot dish plus sandwiches, soup, salad and cookies. Dinner ranges from seafood or Mexican cuisine to turkey or prime rib with a choice of two entrées, vegetables, salad, fresh-baked bread and dessert. The main meal often centers around a particular theme ranging from Hawaiian to Cajun to Western barbeque.

Ride through interesting terrain.

Between meals, guests can nibble from a bowl of fresh fruit or a plate of cookies that are always kept well stocked. The ranch also provides plenty of lemonade, iced tea, coffee, and assorted hot teas to quench your thirst.

A Refreshing Environment For Gatherings

During the fall, winter and spring, the ranch turns its efforts towards corporate business meetings. Rock Springs provides the meeting rooms, the equipment, lodgings and the food service. The ranch only accommodates one group at a time, to insure a productive and distraction free environment. A new 4,400 square foot conference center will be completed in September 1989.

Getting There

To reach Rock Springs, follow U.S. 20 north from Bend for six miles to Tumalo. Turn west on the Tumalo Reservoir Road and follow signs for three miles to the ranch.

RIVERPLACE ALEXIS HOTEL

Address: 1510 Southwest Harbor Way, Portland, OR 97201
Telephone: (503) 228-3233, (800) 227-3233
Location: On the Willamette River in downtown Portland
Host: Celinda Carlisle Knott, General Manager
Room Rates: $140 double, $160 to $500 suites. Weekend rates available.
Credit Cards: American Express, Carte Blanche, Diners Club, Discover, JCB, MasterCard, Visa
Remarks: Continental breakfast included in room rates.

"The RiverPlace Alexis Hotel is a resort in the middle of a city," says general manager Celinda Carlisle Knott. "We offer all the amenities of a big resort, yet we are a small luxury hotel."

The RiverPlace Alexis borders Portland's new riverside esplanade. The clapboard and brick structure combines the pastel elegance of a New England farmhouse with the cozy look of an Amsterdam rowhouse. Lovely window boxes and lively windsocks add a festive flair. The front yard is the Willamette River and a yacht basin which is haven to sailboats, powerboats, and racks of rowing shells. Condos rise above a row of neighboring shops and restaurants — a designer deli, a bookstore "for the soul," and a neighborhood concierge. It is a compact European village with distinct Northwest overtones.

First-Rate Service

The RiverPlace Alexis, which opened in 1985, uniquely fills the needs of the savvy business traveler as well as the discriminating pleasure traveler. It offers the warmth one would expect of a bed and breakfast, yet the sophistication of a fine hotel. Of its 74 guest rooms, 24 are suites. All rooms are spacious and airy and decorated in a specially created palette of colors that brighten even the gloomiest of Northwest days. Periwinkle accents on a pale yellow theme lend a light touch. Thick carpeting, handcrafted rugs, and botanical prints add a homey warmth. Six of the rooms feature a wood burning fireplace. An Italian marble bar, refrigerator and whirlpool bath grace others. Many rooms offer a view of the marina.

"What it all comes down to is service," Celinda says. "Our staff sees guests as their honored family members." From the moment you arrive, when a smiling valet greets you at your car, to check-out time when the bellman calls you by name, the modus operandi is full-on service. Few other hotels would

think to review the guest list in order to have home country flags flying upon the foreign traveler's arrival. Complimentary sherry, cozy terry robes and warm up suits, fresh flowers in all public areas, twice daily maid service with nightly turndown, a multilingual staff, and morning newspaper delivered to the door are but a few of the attentive gestures. A trip to the private sauna and spa begins with the bellman escort from your room. A Continental breakfast (included in the room rate) may be enjoyed in the hotel's Esplanade Restaurant or in your room. Twenty-four hour room service and "cross training" shoes delivered upon request are among the finishing touches.

Ten condo units adjacent to the hotel are available for long term rental (one week at least). All feature river views, fireplaces, washer and dryer, and a complete kitchen, a convenient addition for those longer stays.

The hotel is ideally suited to the needs of the professional. Banquet and meeting rooms accommodate up to 200 for dining and 400 for receptions. while more intimate rooms are designed for smaller groups.

Riverside Dining

The Alexis offers a trio of dining spots: the Esplanade Restaurant, The Patio, and The Bar. The Esplanade, serving breakfast, lunch, and dinner, seats 83 in the bi-level dining room overlooking the marina. Fresh Northwest cuisine is highlighted with a selection of seafoods, poultry and meats. Ragout of prawns and scallops, Dungeness crab with tamari, ginger and scallions, and filet of beef with wild mushrooms and brandy, are but a few of the innovative entrées on a menu that changes with each season.

The Patio serves light patio fare (mesquite-grilled burgers, gourmet sausages, salads) in the summer months. Lunches in The Bar range from the best burger in town to clams and mussels in white wine and herbs. You can enjoy live entertainment five times a week here while contemplating the panoramic view of the river. French Press coffee complete with a tray full of accompaniments and sumptuous desserts can turn into an indulent feast.

A Walking Tour

One of the best ways to see Portland is to merely step out the front door of the RiverPlace Alexis and begin walking. Adjacent to the hotel is Tom McCall Park, a wide green lawn that parallels the Willamette. Jogging trails wind along the riverbank through the park. The nearby Portland Art Museum houses 35 centuries of world art in its extensive collections acquired over the past 90 years. Northwest Coast Indian Art, Asian, West African, American and European art are all exhibited.

Portland's most historic buildings are found in the Skidmore/Old Town Historical District, the largest remaining concentration of 19th century cast

The Fireplace Suite is ideal for entertaining.

iron west of the Mississippi. Cafes, specialty shops and an outdoor market-place add to the area's charm.

Yamhill Marketplace, in the Yamhill Historic District, is a five-level glass atrium containing more than 50 shops. Just north of the Yamhill District is Chinatown. Oriental imports, old and new artifacts, ethnic grocery stores and restaurants are found in these colorful blocks. The RiverPlace Alexis' location makes it ideal for strolling the Esplanade shops or watching the activity on the busy waterfront. Guests may use the RiverPlace Athletic Club with indoor pools, gyms, track, weight room, aerobic program and child watch.

Getting There

To reach the RiverPlace Alexis, follow signs to City Center-Front Street. Take Front Avenue to Market Street. Head south on Market Street following signs to RiverPlace Marina. Stay in the far left lane. Turn left at the first traffic signal onto Montgomery Street. Turn immediately left on Harbor Way. The hotel is at the end of Harbor Way.

GENOA

Address:	2832 Southeast Belmont Street
	Portland, OR 97214
Telephone:	(503) 238-1464
Hosts:	Amelia and Fred Hard
Cuisine:	Northern Italian
Prices:	Seven-course dinner, $35; four-course dinner, $28
Credit Cards:	American Express, Carte Blanche, Diners Club,
	Discover, MasterCard, Visa
Hours:	Seven-course dinner seatings from 6 to 9:30 p.m. on
	the hour and half-hour, four-course dinner seatings
	only at 5:30, 6, 10, and 10:30 p.m.
	Monday through Saturday.

Portland's modest eastside holds a surprising dining find. Genoa, a fine Italian restaurant, hides under an inconspicuous canopy in an unlikely neighborhood. The one-room bistro, painted in deep muted burgundy, exudes a quietly understated elegance. Italian caneback chairs, select antiques, and a decorative Oriental rug accent the unpretentious decor.

Prix Fixe

Genoa is known for its seven-course, fixed price dinner. The approximately two- to three-hour meal takes you on a leisurely tour of Northern Italian cuisine. The four senior cooks rotate duties semi-monthly; each is responsible for researching, designing, testing, and preparing their feasts for a two-week period.

Just as each cook takes pride in the meal design, the servers take pride in the presentation. The deliberate lack of hierarchy in the restaurant management creates an atmosphere of cooperation in which each employee works with a sense of individual responsibility. Present owners Amelia and Fred Hard were also employees of the restaurant before purchasing it.

Northern Italian Extravaganza

Genoa has achieved high ratings from restaurant reviewers. *Oregon Magazine* ranked it one of the 10 best restaurants in the state. The secret: fine, fresh foods and delightful, delicate seasonings.

The meal begins with antipasto, which in summer might be proscuitto and melon or lime-marinated salmon. The winter antipasto is bagna cauda, a hot fondue of cream, anchovy and garlic served with crisp vegetables and homemade sourdough breadsticks for dipping. An innovative soup follows. Homemade pasta, which is always fresh, comes next. A fish course follows, perhaps red snapper with a light white wine and lemon sauce, topped with cinnamon, pine nuts and orange slices, or oysters baked with crème fraiche, mushrooms, bread crumbs and fresh marjoram.

Of seven courses, the only choices to be made are in the entrées and the desserts. Three entrées are offered, including seafood, fowl and meat. Scallops sautéed with capers, shallots and red peppers, veal in a sage cream sauce, or roasted quail with stuffing are just a few entrée possibilities.

Genoa's dazzling dessert tray features over 100 recipes. Coffee, espresso, cappuccino and dessert wines are offered to round out the meal, followed by a selection of fresh fruits.

A lengthy wine list offers Italian, French, California and Northwest wines. Aperitifs may be ordered before the meal.

Getting There

From downtown Portland, go east over the Morrison Street Bridge. The street becomes Belmont. Continue approximately one and one-half miles.

Experience why *Bon Appétit* calls Genoa "uncommonly sophisticated."

HERON HAUS

Address:	2545 N.W. Westover Road, Portland, OR 97210
Telephone:	(503) 274-1846
Host:	Julie Beacon Keppeler, Innkeeper
Room Rates:	$85 to $150 double, five deluxe guest rooms. Includes generous continental breakfast.
Credit Cards:	None
Remarks:	Children 13 and older welcome. No pets. No smoking.

"A woman was chief of all who lived in this region," said Coyote, in an ancient legend of the Yakima nation, "but that was before people were real people." Coyote then issued a proclamation: "Women will no longer be chiefs." The one exception was Tsagaglalal, whose wisdom and goodness persuaded Coyote to transform her into a rock overlooking her village in the Columbia Gorge's Horsethief Canyon. "You shall stay here and watch over the people who lived here," Coyote commanded. "You will see all things."

The story of "She Who Watches" was a familiar one to Julie Beacon Keppeler. Not only was her grandfather, M.M. Hill, one of the original Hood River settlers but her stepfather, Emory Strong, was a leading authority on Columbia River Indians. And if her stepfather was at all inclined to give credence to the Indian myths he collected, Julie was not.

Keppeler had always been a leader in her world, a world in which for 25 years she had performed the traditional role of wife and mother. So when that chapter was complete, Julie found herself back from Hawaii and living in Portland. She was soon helping her parents complete the construction of a multi-million dollar Columbia Gorge Interpretive Center. She accepted the challenge with her characteristic zeal.

Ode to Mother

But one project wasn't enough to keep Julie busy. And as she roamed the hills of Portland, wondering about her next move, she happened up on a tudor-style Victorian that was in dire need of some tender loving care. "I didn't know what I was doing," Julie remembers, "I just knew I had to do it."

She purchased the three-story mansion in July 1986 and stripped and re-wallpapered, varnished old woodwork and pulled up old carpeting to reveal parquet flooring in mint condition. The process continued for more than sixteen months and as she worked day by day, Julie recalled the story of her mother's "guardian angel."

"She was crossing a street one day," she recalls, "when a spectacular white heron flew across the sky. She stopped to watch the bird, and a car appearing out of nowhere came barreling through the intersection not inches from where she stood. Had it not been for that bird, my mother would have been killed." Julie decided to call her house the Heron House and she opened its doors on New Year's Eve, 1987.

Matters of the Heart

"My quest is to maintain a simple elegance," Julie says, "to extend to every guest the kind of comfort and care that would be given to a treasured friend." And so, full of ideas accumulated through her years in Hawaii and Europe, her skills as a hostess and a teacher and her love of the arts, Julie set out to fill Heron Haus with warmth and elegance.

Situated in a quiet residential neighborhood of the Northwest Portland hills, Heron Haus is surrounded by some of Portland's oldest and finest homes. "There just aren't many views like this, "Julie points out, as you gaze at the sparkling city of Portland, its bridges rising over the glistening Willamette River, with Mt. Hood, the sleeping giant, in the distance. Below you, an orange grove bordered by juniper, laurel, holly and rhododendron trees, provides privacy. A free form swimming pool sparkles invitingly.

Guests who are encouraged to make themselves completely at home are free to roam the house's rooms. There's a handsome mahogany bar, TV room complete with high-tech electronics and a provocative crystal chess set in the living room. The Haus' dining room is light, airy and joyful. Julie serves a scrumptious breakfast of coffee and teas, fresh melons and a basket of pumpkin, raisin and cinnamon pastries, date nut and tangy orange rolls.

The relaxed feeling of the Heron Haus extends to the five guest rooms on the second and third floors, all of which have Hawaiian names – Manu, Kulia, Maluhia, Makua and Ko. Decorated in blues, lavenders and rose, each room has a spacious sitting area, large antique bed covered in comfy down quilts and a telephone. You'll enjoy the baths, one of which features a raised spa with a panoramic view of the city. Another features a roomy shower complete with seven pulsating spray spouts.

Portland's Colorful Nob Hill

For those unfamiliar with the neighborhoods of Portland, the bohemian liveliness of the Nob Hill district offers a walk on the wild side. You'll find shops with names like Love Joy Opticians, Rapunzel Hair Design, Katayama Framing, and Luv 'N Stuff Flowers. Entrepreneurship flourishes, from the Nob Hill Business Associates Shuttle to "Coffee People" and a pup that delivers

The main rooms have a majestic view of Portland.

the mail. There is also a tasty selection of eclectic and ethnic restaurants, Seafood Mama, Papa Haydn's and Eat Your Heart Out.

For a more tranquil setting, Portland's International Rose Test Gardens and Japanese Garden are in nearby Washington Park. Forest Park, one of the largest urban forests and arboretums in the United States, is only steps from the Heron Haus door.

Getting There

From Interstate 405, take the Everett Street Exit. Turn onto Glisan, which is a one way street. Turn right on 24th and go three blocks to Johnson. Turn left to Westover Road. Proceed up the incline to the Heron Haus. There are parking spaces by the front door.

THE HEATHMAN HOTEL

Address: SW Broadway at Salmon, Portland, OR 97205
Telephone: (800) 551-0011 for reservations
(503) 241-4100
Host: Mary Arnstad, General Manager
Room Rates: $120 to $140 double. $175 to $160 one- and two-
bedroom suites.
Credit Cards: All major
Remarks: Weekend and specialty packages are available.

At a time when cities across the nation were bursting at their seams, yet ignoring the consequences of traffic and unplanned sprawl, Portland was tearing up freeways and planting parks. At a time when pollution was considered a fact of city life, Portland was turning to hydroelectric power and clean air, establishing a bottle law and restoring the Willamette River to ensure the purest drinking water in the country.

Rock of Revival

As modern spires began appearing on the skyline, the City of Roses encouraged the restoration of the 19th century architectural landmarks. One of these was The Heathman Hotel. The new Heathman Hotel, as it was called when it opened in 1927, was showing the lines of age in 1984. The Heathman's solid ten-story brick exterior now reflects the city's more staid, provincial side of life. But once the doorman closes the glass entry behind you, the hand of interior designer Andrew Delfino takes over, beckoning you into a world of elegant residential comfort.

Satisfying Your Every Whim

The grand foyer has cool marble and polished teakwood. The hotel's subtle oriental flavor is evident throughout, including its Ming pieces and a rare rice paper Japanese print.

The resourceful concierge can assist you with valet parking and transportation, secretaries, interpreters, a waterproof runner's guide, theater tickets, dining reservations and privileged access to nearby athletic clubs.

The Hotel's 152 guest rooms and suites have all been designed with the needs of a discerning traveler in mind. From simple guest rooms to one- and two-bedroom suites, the hotel can offer parlor suites with corner view living rooms

for a variety of hospitality and business functions. There's a room for every need at The Heathman, all beautifully furnished and maintained.

Warm tones of terra cotta, celery and ivory accent the polished hardwood and contemporary rattan furnishings, which are covered in colorful English chintzes. King, queen and twin beds are available and rooms offer every conceivable amenity – color television, 24 hour room service, plush bathrobes, Italian soaps and bath accessories and nightly turndown service to make your stay pleasant, comfortable and refreshingly luxurious.

Uncommon Services

The Heathman's Mezzanine level, soon to be an alfresco bar with tapas-style dining, contains art pieces from the Elizabeth Leach Gallery, as well as a view to the Tea Court below. You'll find seven distinctive reception rooms for high-level business meetings or private entertaining. The Symphony Room, with its fireplace, private service bar, and adjoining entrance to the Arlene Schnitzer Concert Hall, is the perfect location for a pre- or post-event party to taste the excellence of Portland's performing arts. The Heathman's separate kitchen and private pantries can easily accommodate the culinary and service needs for groups of 10 to 150 guests.

In the hotel's social Tea Court, two 17th century oils by Claude Gellee set the tone for the hand polished gumwood panels,, a gracefully curving stairway, arched windows and a Steinway grand piano. This classic setting is perfect for an after dinner nightcap or afternoon tea. Lace-aproned hostesses serve finger sandwiches, scones and pastries along with The Heathman's special blend tea on fine English bone china .

Designer Dining

The Heathman restaurant has an enviable reputation for its local Oregon seafood, freshwater fish, game and other hand selected delicacies. It's snappy, energetic atmosphere is enhanced with Andy Warhol's "Endangered Species" animal art. For more casual fare, there's the Marble Bar, which is only a window away from the Portland's bustling streets.

A few extra steps up the block is the B. Moloch Heathman Bakery & Pub. Its fun-loving decor highlights the work of 19th century French caricaturist, B. Moloch. A ten-ton woodburning oven and specially designed smoke box add to the flavor of the cooking that has won the pub a loyal local following.

In the Center of Things

Portland has been determined to provide a pleasant, rich, diverse pedestrian experience. Many streets have been closed to cars so that the sounds of the city's parks and rivers are more noticeable than the noise of the traffic.

The Tea Court is off the lobby and provides an ideal atmosphere for relaxing.

The South Park area is home not only to The Heathman Hotel but to a light and lively theater district as well. The new Performing Arts Center is beginning its second season with the Portland Center Stage, an offshoot of the award winning Ashland-based Oregon Shakespeare Festival. The Willamette River provides a tranquil backdrop to the park that stretches for miles along its waterline, and reminds you that Portland like The Heathman Hotel, is for those who appreciate versatility.

Getting There

From the north: Take Interstate 5 to the City Center Exit across the Broadway Bridge. Bear left on Broadway and go 16 blocks to the corner of Broadway and Salmon. The Hotel is on the right.

From the south: Take Interstate 5 north to Interstate 405 and continue on to the Salmon Street Exit. Go right on Salmon Street to the corner of Salmon and Broadway and make a right turn to the Hotel.

COLUMBIA GORGE HOTEL

Address: 4000 Westcliff Drive, Hood River, OR 97031
Telephone: (503) 386-5566, (800) 345-1921
Location: On the western outskirts of Hood River, 61 miles east of Portland
Host: Lynne L. LaFountaine, Manager
Room Rates: $115 to $185, double
Credit Cards: American Express, Diners Club, Discover, MasterCard, Visa
Remarks: Rates include "World Famous Farm Breakfast"

The mighty Columbia River surges at its feet. Majestic Mt. Hood protrudes at its back. Phelps Creek, which takes a final dramatic 203-foot leap to join the powerful river below, meanders through its 13 acres of flowered grounds. The Columbia Gorge Hotel has a most spectacular setting indeed.

This elegant inn is as rich with history as it is beauty. Oregon lumber magnate Simon Benson, prime mover behind the Columbia River Gorge Scenic Highway project and builder of Portland's Benson Hotel, saw the potential. In 1921, he opened the Columbia Gorge Hotel, a 42-room, three story inn boasting "all with bath" and the state's only ballroom east of Portland.

Soon, the magic was felt and the hotel's reputation grew. In the midst of the Jazz Age, the Columbia Gorge Hotel became a favorite retreat for the "idle rich." Famous guests, such as Rudolph Valentino and Clara Bow, were said to have stayed here, and some even had rooms named after them.

The hotel changed hands several times over the years, and eventually became victim of the nation's economic climate. In 1952 it became a retirement home, and suffered sorely from neglect. 1978 brought new owners, the hotel was restored, and its renewed grandeur re-earned it the title "Waldorf of the West."

All That Jazz

The hotel's exterior, with red tile roof, mustard yellow stucco walls and shuttered windows, is somewhat reminiscent of a Spanish monastery. Entering the foyer, however, the feeling of the Flapper Era begins to take hold. Massive plastered beams, a glittery chandelier, swinging French doors and glass doorknobs take you back 60 years. Just off the lobby is the Valentino Lounge, a plush gathering place for sipping cocktails and enjoying music.

All 42 rooms are different. Antique furniture and authentic replicas (goose-neck rockers, overstuffed chairs) create a warm uncluttered look. A few rooms offer a fireplace, another features a wood canopy bed. Rooms 239 and 339 are directly above the Wah-Gwin-Gwin Falls.

The hotel has become a respected host to corporate and private groups: the Benson Ballroom, with its removable dance floor, is ideal for meetings, banquets and weddings; the Falls Room is well suited for smaller groups.

Famous Food

The Columbia Gorge Hotel prides itself on its trademarked "World Famous Farm Breakfast" which, by all counts, is enough food to provide sustenance for a week. Upward of 17 varieties of fruits are displayed on individual dishes. Next, a steaming baked apple arrives, followed closely by a crock of oatmeal. Three eggs, ham, sausage links, bacon and hash browns are served with country biscuits and the famed "honey from the sky." Save room for the stack of hotcakes that complete the meal because, as the menu says, it's not a choice — you get it all. Coffee, tea and chilled champagne are all available.

The dining room overlooks the river. At night, in the soft candlelight, it becomes a romantic spot for enjoying a leisurely meal and watching the lights on the opposite shore. The excellent service is accentuated by tableside flambés and sautés. The varied menu includes Oregon favorites such as Columbia River sturgeon and rack of eastern Oregon lamb which Chef Patricio Herrera prepares in a creative fashion. Peppercorn filet medallions and Columbia River salmon round out the entrée offerings. The wine list, with over 400 offerings, highlights wines from the Pacific Northwest, in addition to a wide selection of California and French vintages.

Gorge Yourself

The hotel is a wonderful base for the many activities found in this region. The Gorge has become a mecca for windsurfers in the last few years — westerly winds blow up to 60 miles per hour and an opposing current flows up to six knots, creating ideal conditions for skilled board sailors. From the hotel and other vantage points, you can watch the vibrantly colored sails jumping and jibing through the waves. Bonneville Lock and Dam, the first hydroelectric powerhouse in the area, offers a visitor's center along the Washington shore of the Columbia. Watch grain barges navigate the locks and, from April to October, see salmon climb fish ladders on their upstream journey. For a closer look at the river, the 145-foot sternwheeler *Columbia Gorge*, an authentic replica of an 1800s paddlewheeler, departs and returns to Cascade Locks three times each day.

High adventure is found in fishing for Columbia Gorge sturgeon that can reach lengths of 15 feet in their century-long lifespan. Whitewater rafting,

The restaurant provides wonderful views down into the gorge.

horseback riding, and hiking are other activities in the area. The hotel will gladly arrange these for guests.

In the winter, the ski areas of Mt. Hood are easily reached from the hotel for a day of either cross-country or down hill.

In spring, white apple blossoms blanket the slopes. By fall, rich harvests are en route to packing sheds. Try driving the Mount Hood loop, Oregon 35, and climb through orchards to supreme vantage points of the Columbia River below. Cross 4,157-foot Barlow Pass along one of the routes used by Oregon Trail pioneers in the 1840s. In spring, wild pink rhododendrens abound, in fall, a profusion of vibrant autumn colors splash the hillside.

Getting There

Take Interstate 84 east from Portland and turn off at Exit 62. Cross the highway and turn left on Westcliff Drive. The hotel is ahead on your right. Amtrak offers service from Portland on the *Pioneer*, and the hotel will arrange transportation from Hood River station.

THE SHELBURNE INN AND THE SHOALWATER RESTAURANT

Address:	Pacific Highway 103 and 45th St., Seaview, WA 98644
Telephone:	(206) 642-2442 (inn), (206) 642-4142 (restaurant)
Location:	One mile south of Long Beach on Long Beach Peninsula
Hosts:	David Campiche and Laurie Anderson, Innkeepers; Tony and Ann Kischner, Restaurateurs
Room Rates:	$69 to $135 double. Midweek off-season lodging and dining packages available October through June
Credit Cards:	American Express, Diners Club, MasterCard, Visa
Remarks:	Complimentary country breakfast with room. No pets.
Hours:	Lunch noon to 2:30 p.m, dinner 5:30 to 9:30 p.m. Sunday brunch 10 a.m. to 2:30 p.m. Closed Wednesdays Oct.–June 15.

The first thing you notice upon entering the Shelburne Inn is that turn-of-the-century motif is so thoroughly intact, you might just be tempted to tap your wrist watch and wonder if this is a scene from "Somewhere in Time."

The Shelburne, built in 1896, is the oldest continually-operating lodging establishment in the state. Located on Washington's twenty-eight-mile Long Beach Peninsula, the inn was originally a mecca for Oregonians escaping the heat. Summer guests would steam along the river on the paddlewheeler *T.J. Potter* to the Port of Ilwaco, then hop a narrow gauge rail to Seaview. The existing structure, now on the National Register of Historic Places, has undergone a series of changes, including the 1911 uniting of two buildings from opposing sides of the street in the spot where the inn now rests.

David Campiche, a Seaview native, watched the inn deteriorate for several years until he and his wife, Laurie Anderson, decided to purchase it in 1977 and begin renovation. Both were knowledgeable in antiques, and together they scoured England and Holland for the quality pieces now filling the inn. In 1983, a major expansion of the lower level was completed, and Art Nouveau stained glass windows were integrated into the structure. A new wing, built in 1986, added five guest rooms, bringing the total to sixteen.

Quiet Victorian Retreat

Thirteen of the rooms in the three story inn have private baths; two are suites. Hand-stitched quilts, crocheted pillow shams, brass bedsteads, and marble-topped dressers add distinction to each room. Gathered artwork from Europe as well as locally grace the walls. Most rooms open onto verandas appointed with potted flowers.

A couple of large tables in the lobby are set for breakfast. The country-style feast is complimentary with a room. David and Laurie and their staff devote much of their energies to create a breakfast that *Washington Magazine* recently pronounced "the best in the state." Their breakfast has also been featured in *Gourmet* and *Food and Wine.*

First-Rate Dining

The Shoalwater Restaurant shares what owner Tony Kischner describes as a "symbiotic relationship" with the Shelburne Inn. Linked by a couple of doorways, a strong friendship, and a common spirit, the two businesses work in harmony to provide a complete dining and lodging experience. The dining room decor is consistent with that of the inn.

Tony, formerly manager of Seattle's prestigious Other Place, and his wife Ann joined David and Laurie in 1981. Tony blends the best of his international upbringing with his restaurant training to create a superb dining experience. Northwest foods are showcased in a seasonally varied menu. "People travel for miles to have our mussel chowder," he says.

Fresh Willapa Bay oysters are featured, both on the half-shell as appetizers, and pan fried for an entrée. Columbia River white sturgeon in an inventive Oriental marinade is grilled to perfection. Roast Oregon duck is surrounded by dried Washington cherry and Cabernet sauce; A Northwest seafood stew brings together the best local fin and shellfish in a saffron-flavored stock. A number of menu items are starred to identified those available as low calorie or low cholestral. Ann's homemade bread accompanies the meal, and her dessert tray merits the rave reviews and awards she has received.

Lunch and Sunday brunch are of equivalent quality, and again utilize fresh in-gredients and culinary expertise. Tony is proud of his extensive wine list, the winner of the presigious *Wine Spectator* Award of Excellence in 1988.

The most recent addition to the Shelburne/Shoalwater duo is the Heron & Beaver Pub. Northwest microbreweries on tap are spotlighted, as are single-malt Scotch whiskys. The full bar offers an intimate spot for cocktails, or for a meal of light pub fare. Stuffed pub buns, and daily pasta specials are among the offerings served in the cozy gathering place.

Year-Round Destination

A favorite time on the Long Beach Peninsula is winter, when big storms hammer their way along the coast. Bundle up and beachcomb for Japanese fishing floats, driftwood and shells. Drive for miles along the state-owned beach where kite flying and photography are favorite oceanside pastimes. Steelhead fishing is prime in winter, while the summer months bring the salmon to the mouth of the Columbia River. Loomis Lake and others nearby

The nationally acclaimed Shoalwater Restaurant is well worth the trip.

teem with trout and bass. Horseback riding, tennis and golf are all found within easy reach of the inn. Curio shops, museums and art galleries, too, await exploration. The southwest corner of the state is on the bird migration route and tens of thousands of waterfowl and shorebirds are seen skimming the beach.

Long Island rests under the protected arm of the peninsula in Willapa Bay. A 274-acre grove of red cedars is one of the last remaining reproducing climax forests that first sprouted during a dramatic West Coast climate change 4,000 years ago. Cedars reach 11 feet in diameter, and average 150 feet in height. Tours are available to this island, which is also home to elk, geese and heron.

Getting There

From Seattle, take I-5 south to Olympia, then Highway 8 and 12 to Montesano. Follow Highway 101 south to Seaview. From the Oregon coast, follow U.S. 101 across the Astoria bridge and turn left to Ilwaco. Head north for two miles until you reach Seaview.

ALEXIS HOTEL SEATTLE

Address: 1007 First Avenue, Seattle, WA 98104
Telephone: (206) 624-4844, (800) 426-7033 outside Washington
Location: Two blocks from the waterfront in downtown Seattle
Host: Noel Burk, General Manager
Room Rates: $135 to $150 double, suites $115.
Weekend rates available.
Credit Cards: American Express, Carte Blanche, Diners Club, MasterCard, Visa
Remarks: Children under 12 stay free. Private dining rooms available.

The Alexis Hotel is a luxury hotel of European inspiration. Captivatingly quiet, the downtown Seattle auberge is elegantly simple and simply elegant.

The handsome building housing the hotel was originally a 1901 office building designed by Max Umbrecht for prominent Seattle businessman James W. Clise. It headquartered Clise's firms for about 15 years, but in 1917 he moved on and the Globe Building suffered a six-decade period of decline. The building survived the Depression years as a home to the public market, became a parking garage, and in 1980 became part of a six-square-block area undergoing revitalization by Paul Schell's Cornerstone Development Company. The Alexis, totally renovated by the noted Baumgardner Architects, has earned a place in the National Register of Historic Places.

Service Counts

Elegance and luxury aside, what the Alexis Hotel really stands on is its service. The hotel was rated first in Seattle according to the presigious *Zagat Guide*, included ranking for overall quality, room quality, dining and service. Limosine service within the downtown area and access to a local health club are available as well.

The Alexis Seattle has 54 rooms in 18 room styles. Parlor suites, executive one-bedroom suites, and fireplace suites are the more spacious. Many rooms overlook the inner courtyard. Some have a jacuzzis, wet bar and refrigerator. Televisions are tucked away in beautiful armoires. Italian and Alaskan marble accent the pastel colors used throughout the hotel. All rooms have extension phones, plush terry robes, fine soaps and lotions, and down pillows. There is a steam room on the third floor, and two lighted tennis courts on the roof. Among the services, Alexis guests find lobby sherry service, twice daily maid service, steam room, choice of newspaper, and shoeshine service.

Alexis Style Dining

The Alexis Hotel Seattle opened their own Cafe Alexis in the manner they know best: small, polished and perfect in detail, yet gracious, warm and welcoming. The restaurant seats 28 in its intimate room and serves lunch and dinner. Private dining for breakfast is also available. Rotating exhibits by Northwest artists grace the walls. The menu changes weekly; specials change daily. International flavors are added to traditional dishes, mixed with Northwest freshness, and served simply and beautifully.

The Alexis Hotel's newest restaurant, 92 Madison, features an extensive juice bar with exotic fruit smoothies and liquados. Breakfasts, from the traditional continental to scrambled eggs with Italian sausage or diced apples and cheddar cheese, 5 grain cereal oatmeal and buckwheat flapjacks are sure to please. The restaurant is a comfortable attractive place for casual lunches or private banquets in the evening. The food is familiar – pot pies, pasta, meat loaf, ribeye steak – but made with far more care and special ingredients than you'd have time to do at home. The Alexis Hotel also features one of Seattle's three cajun restaurants. A popular spot, the Cajun Corner is known for its authentic Cajun food.

The Bookstore ... A Bar offers cocktail service as well as light lunches and innovative appetizers. Housed in a former bookstore, it features micro-brewery beers and hot, soft pretzels. It is a friendly place where regulars are known by name and not-so-regulars are easily engaged in conversation. International newspapers, magazines and books are available for browsing or for purchase. After all, it is a bookstore . . . and a bar.

Seattle's Heart

The Alexis Seattle is located near the center of a vital metropolis. The business and financial district is only blocks away, as are the airline office and governmental centers. The world famous Pike Place Market is a short walk north along the busy waterfront area. There is also an Australian trolly car to tour the waterfront.

Head south from the front door of the hotel to reach Pioneer Square, the heart of Seattle's historic district. The area had its beginnings in 1852, and many of the old brick buildings have been restored to their original state. Shops, restaurants, exotic boutiques and art galleries now occupy the handsome structures. The Underground Tour takes you under present-day Pioneer Square for a glimpse of Seattle in the 1890s, before a devastating fire burned it to the ground. The southern border of the Pioneer Square district is the Kingdome, where many of Seattle's major sporting events are held. Nearby is the hub of the Asian community, the International District, where dozens of ethnic shops and restaurants line the streets.

92 Madison is just off the lobby.

Just as Pioneer Square is Seattle's historic heart, the Seattle Center is its cultural heart. The 74-acre legacy of the 1962 World's Fair is site of the 605-foot Space Needle, Seattle's most distinctive landmark. An elevator swiftly carries passengers to the observation level from which a 360-degree view of the city and environs can be seen. Both mountain ranges, the Cascades to the east and Olympics to the west, Puget Sound, Lake Washington and Lake Union, and the myriad of bridges, parks and barges may be seen from this bird's-eye view. The restaurant, one level below, revolves one full turn per hour, so while you dine there is an ever-changing mural of sights. The Center is home to a continuing series of visiting cultural, art and science exhibits.

Getting There

From northbound I-5, take the Madison Street Exit. Head west on Madison to 1st Avenue. From southbound I-5, take the Stewart Steet Exit to 1st Avenue. Turn left and continue to Madison. The hotel is on the corner of 1st and Madison. Valet parking is available for $8 per day.

ROVER'S

Address:	2808 E. Madison, Seattle, WA 98112
Telephone:	(206) 325-7442
Hosts:	Thierry and Kathy Rautureau, Diane Stein
Prices:	Menu de gustation $34.50. Entrees $18.25 to $19.75.
Credit Cards:	American Express, Carte Blanche, Diners Club, Discover, MasterCard, Visa,
Hours:	Monday through Saturday, 5 p.m. to close.

Tucked behind the upscale shops of Madison Valley, is an unassuming beige house, home of Rover's restaurant. It is not razzle-dazzle and flash that make Rover's one of Seattle's great restaurants. Rather, Rover's reputation relies on the fine quality of its food, service and atmosphere.

Operated for the last two years by owners Thierry Rautureau and Diane Stein, Rover's has earned well-deserved respect from Seattle's restaurant critics and patrons. The restaurant's atmosphere is one of subtle sophistication. Quiet peach walls are hung with works by local artists. (The show changes every few months.) Muted lighting, candles and white linens lend an elegant tone. Strains of jazz or classical music add to the pleasant atmosphere of the three small dining rooms. Rover's retains such a loyal following that reservations are required for most evenings.

Rover's culinary craft is piloted by the fiery young Frenchman, Thierry Rautureau. Thierry began cooking at the age of 14. He has been developing his art ever since. The range of his expertise has been influenced by several apprenticeships that were served in France. It is layered with the Asian influences reflective of his five years in Los Angeles. Thierry incorporates the bounty of fresh Northwest ingredients with his natural flair for combining flavors. A bountiful kitchen garden provides the chef with three dozen varieties of herbs and edible flowers to enhance his culinary skills. The result is food he refers to as "Northwest contemporary with a French accent."

The co-owners of Rover's met in Los Angeles, where Thierry was guest instructor at the Epicurean Cooking School. Diane, then a student, filled in as assistant. While working together, the two made plans for opening their own restaurant. They make a very creative team. Thierry is the chef. Diane creates many of the pastries and works the books. Thierry's wife, Kathy Encell Rautureau, is the hostess and flower arranger.

Chef's Choice

To feel perfectly pampered and catered to, order Rover's *menu de gustation*—Thierry's prix fixe meal. Changing daily, this five-course dinner features the finest available ingredients. "Trust the chef to select for you," says Thierry, "then sit back and relax." It is not uncommon to see Thierry circulate among the tables, conversing with his guests and offering wine selections.

The á la carte menu also changes with the seasons and the whims of the chef. Appetizers may include duck ravioli with shitake mushrooms and a light rosemary sauce, or pan fried goat cheese with roasted bell peppers and goat cheese sauce. A favorite salad is the warm duck salad with walnuts, mixed greens, and a fine raspberry vinegar dressing.

Rautureau's versatility and imagination are reflected in his entree selections. Grilled king salmon may be teamed with an oyster mushroom and ginger sauce capitalizing on his fascination with Oriental flavorings. Washington rabbit is presented with flageolet beans and a balsamic vinegar sauce, and roasted pheasant may appear with fresh morels and a black peppercorn sauce. Thierry is often praised for his subtle sauces that enhance the food rather than camouflage the natural goodness. Desserts include delicious bavarois of yogurt with fresh berries and fruit coulis, and creme brulee. An extensive wine list with a range in price offers selections to complement any meal.

Getting There

Follow Madison Street east from downtown Seattle. Rover's is in a courtyard off E. Madison and 28th Street.

Diane and Thierry are a very innovative team.

DOMINIQUE'S PLACE

Address: 1927 43rd Avenue East, Seattle, WA 98112
Telephone: (206) 329-6620
Hosts: Dominique and Chou Chou Place
Cuisine: French
Room Rates: $5.75 to $15 for lunch crepes and entrees, dinner
                          entrees $11.50 to $22, five-course dinner $32.
Credit Cards: American Express, Diners, Club, Discover,
                          MasterCard, Visa
Hours: Lunch Monday through Friday 11:30 a.m. to 2:30
                          p.m. (summertime only), dinner 5 to 10:30 p.m., until
                          11:30 p.m. Friday and Saturday

"The secret to sauces is fullness of flavor," says owner Dominique Place. "Making sauces is very much like making a fine wine." Dominique's sensitive approach to sauces is but one reason his restaurant is a rare dining find.

French born Dominique Place received extensive culinary training in France. Early in his career he accumulated an impressive collection of awards and distinctions, making it clear he was destined to be a skillful chef. A Seattle restaurateur discovered Dominique and brought him to the States. Dominique and his wife Chou Chou later opened this restaurant in Madison Park.

The small bistro is snuggled into a corner of this chic Seattle neighborhood. Neighbored by boutiques, flower shops and fine gift stores, it gazes directly out onto Lake Washington and beyond to the Cascade Mountains. In summer, linen cloaked tables line the sidewalk under the restaurant's blue canvas awnings. In winter, steaming windows tell of cozy evenings inside by the fire.

Fresh and Varied

Dominique makes several trips per week to the local markets in search of fresh ingredients.He designs four- and five-course menus which change frequently. These *prix fixe* meals showcase a well-rounded variety of specialties. The five-course meal typically begins with an appetizer; for instance, sautéed rabbit liver with a light raspberry sauce, or salmon and smoked salmon paté with a light herb dressing. A salad selection follows: mixed green with marinated scallops, prawns and geoduck; or spinach and lettuce with bacon, mushrooms and goat cheese dressing. A palate cleanser of champagne and fruit ice is next, followed by a choice of three or four entrées such as roasted squab with persimmon sauce or sautéed duck breast with pear and ginger sauce. A Grand Dessert Maison, "chef's fantasy," caps off the meal.

Dominique's à la carte menu offers unique selections, from lamb rack medallions served with a rosemary cream and mustard seed sauce, to crepes filled with chicken fillets and vegetables in plum sauce. Full-meal salads, soups, and a plate of cheeses are among the à la carte choices. Crepes are a specialty here, and are served in a number of ways. An exotic flambé of raspberries, chocolate, and ice cream crepes is the perfect end to a satisfying meal.

Lunches consist of a slimmed down version of the dinner menu. A light salmon with sorrel sauce is always a favorite, as is a mixed green salad with orange and praline dressing and sweetbreads. Fresh bread is delivered daily.

An extensive wine list offers selections designed to enhance the meal. French and California wines dominate the cellars.

Getting There

Heading north on I-5, take the Madison Avenue Exit in downtown Seattle and continue east until it ends on the shore of Lake Washington. Dominique's is one building down from the corner of 43rd and Madison, or take the Montlake Exit off 520 to Washington Blvd. Through the Arboretum to Madison Ave. Take left on Madison and continue to Lake Washington.

Enjoy Dominique's salmon paté.

INN AT THE MARKET

Address:	86 Pine Street, Seattle, WA 98101
Telephone:	(206) 443-3600, (800) 446-4484 (outside of Seattle)
Location:	Downtown, in Pike Place Market
Host:	Connie Schneider, General Manager
Room Rates:	$90 to $155 double; suites from $190, $15 for each additional person
Credit Cards:	American Express, Carte Blanche, Discover, MasterCard, Visa, JCB
Remarks:	Children under 16 stay free in parents' room, nonsmoking and handicapped rooms available

Throw open your windows. Savor the heady aromas of coffee, fresh baked goodies and spices wafting up from the Pike Place Market. Listen to the sonorous sounds as the ferry from Bainbridge Island noses into its dock on the waterfront. Gaze westward across Elliott Bay and soak in the last rays of an orange sun silhouetting the jagged peaks of the Olympic Mountains. These, and more, are part of the sensory extravaganza that will be part of your stay at Seattle's Inn at the Market.

Uniquely Seattle

The Inn at the Market offers a unique experience. Its location in the middle of the vital original public market is a much-coveted spot. This neighborhood hotel, one which will feel like home, is conveniently situated in a thriving portion of a large city.

The inn combines comfortable country decor with a host of amenities; complimentary downtown limosine service, refrigerators, coffee makers with fresh ground coffee delivered daily, and evening turn down service with complimentary chocolates. A basket of market-selected amenities awaits in the spacious, tiled bathrooms. For the health conscious, a full-service health club offered to guests at a nominal charge, is just one block away.

Of the 65 guest rooms, 45 offer a view of Puget Sound, the Olympic Mountains, the garden courtyard or the market itself. Three parlor suites on the northwest corner offer the best vantage points. All rooms have floor to ceiling bay windows that open. One-bedroom suites can be converted into two-bedroom townhouses with parlor and connecting bedroom on one level, and second bedroom upstairs. A fifth-floor rooftop deck offers a 180-degree view of Mount Rainer, Elliott Bay and the Pike Place Market below.

Conference and reception rooms are available for groups. Boardroom style meetings can accomodate up to 20 around an oak conference room table, while the same room reception style can handle 50-70 guests.

In the Inn

Select shops and services front the Inn's courtyard. The Comfort Zone Relaxation Spa offers massage therapy, whirlpool, float tank and suntanning, all of which may be billed to your room. The Gravity Bar offers healthy and exotic food and juices created from the market's fresh produce. Baked goods, fresh fruits, granola, warm cereals, and a creative "Eggs Crescent" are available. Another true Seattle treasure is found at the Inn — Cafe Dilettante. The famed chocolaterie provides speciality soups and sandwiches, espresso and desserts. A wine bar features Northwest wines as well as champagnes from around the world.

A Little Village

Stepping out the door of the Inn at the Market, one has the sense of being in a small village. Pike Place Market is an old-time farmer's market where you stroll past fresh fish stalls, vegetable stands and delicatessens amidst a chorus of voices calling out in a dozen languages. In 1971 the market was saved from the wrecking ball and became the focus of the Pike Place Market Historic District, a seven-acre area that is the symbolic heart of Seattle.

Seattle on Foot and Afloat

The Inn is ideally situated for shopping or exploring downtown Seattle on foot. From the shops around the market to the major downtown boutiques and department stores, it is only six blocks. Business travelers will find Seattle's major office buildings a short walk away as well. The symphony, repertory theater, opera and ballet are all easily accessible. A movie theater in the market shows foreign and local films. A corner newsstand sells tabloids in several languages and magazines on most any subject imaginable. Neighboring art galleries display a variety of local and imported talent.

Descending the stairs from the market, known as the Pike Hill Climb, you will arrive on Seattle's waterfront. Seafood restaurants, marine supply stores, import stores, the Seattle Aquarium and Omni Dome Theater line the busy wharfs. A tramway runs parallel to the water, offering easy access to the entire length of the district. Harbor tours are available from a number of operators along these piers.

Washington State is proud of its unique ferry system. Passengers and cars travel across Elliott Bay and Puget Sound to the "bedroom islands" of Bainbridge and Vashon, and to the mainland port of Bremerton. Take a ride from Pier 56 to Winslow, on Bainbridge Island, for a half-hour cruise.

Many of the rooms overlook Elliott Bay and the Pike Place Market.

Winslow offers a fine selection of shops and restaurants, and makes a pleasant afternoon or evening jaunt. Most Seattlites agree, there are few better spots from which to view the sunset over the Olympic Mountains than from the sundeck of the ferry.

For a slightly longer trip pack a picnic basket and take the ferry to Bremerton. The roundtrip ride will take you through the narrow pass on the South end of Bainbridge Island.

Getting There

Follow First Avenue through downtown Seattle to either Pine Street or Stewart Street. You may enter the hotel from either one. Parking with a fee is available at several nearby lots. Parking passes may be obtained at the front desk during check in.

ADRIATICA

Address:	1107 Dexter North, Seattle, WA 98109
Telephone:	(206) 285-5000
Hosts:	Jim and Connie Malevitsis, Owners and Managers
Cuisine:	Mediterranean
Prices:	Entrees $11 to $17
Credit Cards:	American Express, MasterCard, Visa
Hours:	Sunday through Thrusday 5:30 to 10 p.m, Friday and Saturday until 11 p.m.; bar is oepn 5 p.m. to 1 a.m. Sunday through Thursday, until 2 a.m. on Friday and Saturday

Adriatica is located in a remodeled 1920s stucco and clapboard house on a cliff above the south end of Seattle's Lake Union. The Mediterranean restaurant's Greek owner and maitre d' Jim Malevitsis came to this country over 30 years ago. The authentic atmosphere and cuisine belie his European origins. With his wife Connie, who handles the books and menu planning, Jim created the restaurant out of a love for good ethnic cuisine.

The kitchen occupies the first floor of the three story restaurant; the dining room is on the second. The bar on the third floor provides the most dramatic view. Full course meals are served in the dining room, while the bar features a selection of appetizers and light suppers. The outside deck is a popular gathering spot in warm weather.

The main dining room is divided into small, cozy rooms carpeted in "Adriatic blue." Jim's photographs of European scenes and original Greek watercolors set a Mediterranean theme, while white linens and candlelight lend a romantic tone to the warm atmosphere.

L'Heure Bleue

"My favorite time here is what the French call 'l'heure bleue'," Jim. said "At dusk the lights are coming on around Lake Union, and there is a special quality to the natural light.".

Mediterranean Cuisine

Chef Nancy Flume prepares an array of seafoods and traditional Mediterranean dishes utilizing only the highest quality ingredients. Two or three fresh seafood items are served nightly: white king salmon, halibut and petrale sole are grilled with garlic, olive oil, lemon juice and white wine. Seafood souvlaki (grilled prawns and scallops), is basted with cumin, lime and red chile butter.

Meat entrées include raznijici (lamb marinated in zinfandel wine with rosemary and garlic), and filet mignon basted with rosemary, Marsala and garlic butter. A favorite pasta dish is pensotti (large ravioli) filled with spinach, chard and ricotta topped with a walnut sauce.

Traditional Greek salads such as Horiatiki (a Greek village salad with cucumber, tomato, feta, Greek olives and peppers) or a special Belgian endive salad with toasted walnuts, Roquefort and cilantro add to the meal.

A selection of desserts such as chocolate decadence with raspberry sauce or ricotta mouse with chocolate and brandy are the perfect finale to the meal.

Many guests elect to make a full meal of appetizers in the bar. Roasted whole garlic served with croutons and goat cheese is a signature dish.

Getting There

From I-5 take the Mercer Street Exit. Follow signs to Seattle Center, cross Westlake, turn right on Roy. Continue two blocks to Dexter, then turn right on Dexter. The restaurant is three blocks north on the left. From downtown go north on 4th or 6th avenues to Denny. Turn right on Denny, then left on Dexter. The restaurant is nine blocks north on the left side. Parking is available on the south side of the restaurant.

Dine overlooking the waters of Lake Union.

CAFE JUANITA

Address:	9702 Northeast 120th Place, Kirkland, WA 98034
Telephone:	(206) 823-1505
Host:	Peter Dow, Owner
Cuisine:	Northern Italian
Prices:	Entrees $11.25 to $17.50
Credit Cards:	MasterCard, Visa
Hours:	6 p.m. to 10 p.m. daily
Remarks:	Reservations suggested

Peter Dow describes himself as a "closet Italian." He is, in fact, owner of one of the Pacific Northwest's finest Italian restaurants — Cafe Juanita. Peter is also chief wine maker for the house label "Cavatappi," which is produced in his full-scale on-premises winery and served in the restaurant.

Natural Setting

Cafe Juanita is situated on the Juanita Creek in the small community of Juanita, in Kirkland near the northeastern tip of Lake Washington. Formerly a modest brick home, the restaurant is enveloped by willow, maple, and blue spruce trees. The natural setting is carried out inside as well, with muted lighting and warm beige tones set against a hardwood floor.

Buon Appetito

Unobtrusive chalkboards list the ever-changing list of entrées. Before you've reached the third item, someone is at your table to recite the menu in detail, taking time to colorfully describe each dish. Cafe Juanita's innovative offerings proudly exploit seasonal foods.

Begin with an appetizer such as steamed mussels or fresh scallops in white wine, garlic and herbs, puntenesca (sun dried tomatoes, olives, capers and garlic over a delicate penne pasta) or smoked salmon on spaghettini that is made fresh at the Cafe daily.

Cafe Juanita offers eight to ten entrées nightly. A fresh fish selection, such as ahi or swordfish grilled with leeks, lemon, and garlic, is generally available. Other entrées include pollo ai pistacchi (chicken breast baked with proscuitto and parmesan in a pistacchio cream sauce) or piccioni (squab stuffed with Italian sausage and veal in a red wine and tomato sauce). Meat selections may be maiale arrosto (pork loin chops marinated in garlic, olive oil, juniper berries and rosemary), or lasagne (Italian sausage, spinach, and red sauce).

Entrées are followed by a dessert cart featuring homemade specialities, port and liqueurs. Cafe Juanita's own machine churns out fresh fruit gelatos.

Beneath the wisteria in the back yard, there is a small patio that holds only five tables. On summer weekend evenings, Peter may host a special barbeque, however, he won't know until that day if the weather is suitable.

A Focus on Wine

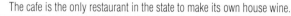

Peter's "Cavatappi" production is reaching 500 cases per year. Known primarily for his sauvignon blanc, this year Peter is introducing the first Italian nebbiolo grown in Washington. He also bottles a small amount of muscat canelli, his special dessert wine. Cafe Juanita also stocks more than 250 Italian wines. This prodigious cellar won an award from *Wine Spectator* as "One of the greatest wine lists in America."

Getting There

From Interstate 405 northbound, take Exit 20A and head west on Northeast 116th Street. In approximately two miles, you will reach the main intersection of Juanita (116th and 98th Avenue Northeast). Continue through the intersection one more block to 97th and turn right. The restaurant is one block straight ahead on the left.

The cafe is the only restaurant in the state to make its own house wine.

THE HERBFARM

Address:	32804 Issaquah-Fall City Road, Fall City, WA 98024
Telephone:	(206) 784-2222
Hosts:	Lola, Bill and Ron Zimmerman and Carrie Van Dyck
Hours:	9 a.m. to 5 p.m. weekdays and 9 a.m. to 6 p.m.weekends mid-March through Christmas. Winter hours, Thursday to Sunday, 10 a.m. to 4 p.m.
Prices:	6-course luncheon program $29.95 per person. Classes free to $22.00.
Remarks:	Free class schedule and catalog. Reservations required for luncheon.

Thirty minutes east of Seattle, where swelling hills announce the beginning of the Cascade range, sets the Herbfarm on a dozen fertile acres between the Snoqualmie and Raging rivers. Here you'll discover over 200,000 potted herb plants in 450 different varieties. Wander among sixteen display gardens while the aromatic country store beckons with a selection of books, dried wreaths, herbal soaps, dried herbs, seeds, and teas. At the farm you'll also find herb-related classes as well as a charming restaurant serving innovative cuisine.

The Herbfarm began as Lola Zimmerman's hobby. One day Lola, who enjoyed growing herbs, parked an old wheelbarrow full of plants under the walnut tree by the street. She left an honor jar of quarters for change, and soon found herself with a growing business. Fifteen years later, Lola and her husband Bill have been joined by their son Ron and his wife Carrie Van Dyck.

A good place to begin your visit to The Herbfarm is with a hosted tour of the walk-through theme gardens. The "Herbal Identification Garden" shows you herbs as they'll be when they mature at your home. At the "Shakespeare Garden," the Zimmerman's have planted herbs mentioned in Shakespeare's plays. Each is marked with the appropriate quote from the bard. The "Good Cooks Garden" entices you to try fresh herbs in your cooking. An "Oregon Trail Garden" grows all the herbs considered essential by pioneering women opening the west. After a look from the rustic gazebo, the guide ends the tour at the "Garden of Thyme" with the irresistible phrase, "It's thyme for lunch."

Fresh From the Garden Luncheons

Those who've secured reservations now enter the charming dining room where tables are set with crocheted place mats and moss-green "cabbage leaf" underplates. Behind the tiled counter in the kitchen, owner-chef Ron Zimmerman and staff are ready to start you on a 2 1/2 hour culinary adventure. As the 6-course extravaganza unfolds, Ron, Carrie, and crew interject bits of herbal lore, share culinary expertise, and generously divulge their recipes.

Menus are ever-changing as vegetables mature in the farm's gardens and as local fish and game come into season. Your meal might begin with a Prelude of Herbal Mousses in a Brown Hen's Egg to be followed by Spring Asparagus with Wild Morels and Caraway Greens. An intermezzo of palate-clearing Rose Geranium and Sweet Cicely Sorbet might lead to Salmon with Lemon Verbena and Tuberous Begonia Sauce, followed by The Herbfarm's Salad From the Meadow's Edge—an artistic medley bursting withover 30 herbs, seasonal greens, and edible flowers. The day's feast could conclude with Lovage Ice Cream with Purple Sage Sauce, coffee, and your choice of over 17 herbal teas. A maximum of 25 lucky people are hosted Fridays, Saturdays, and Sundays from late April through Christmas. Reservations are necessary.

The Herbfarm also presents over 175 classes each year on herbs for gardening, crafts, and cooking. A complete and fascinating schedule is available. In addition, the farm mail orders most of its products, many of which are listed in its twice-annual catalogues. Ask for a copy.

Getting There

Take Interstate 90 east from Seattle to Exit 22 (Preston-Fall City). Go through Preston toward Fall City. At the "Y" in the road after three miles, go over the green bridge onto 328th S.E. Follow signs one-half mile further.

Herb plants, shopping, gardens, 175 classes and fine dining await you at The Herbfarm..

BIRCHFIELD MANOR

Address:	2018 Birchfield Road, Yakima, WA 98901
Telephone:	(509) 452-1960
Hosts:	Wil and Sandy Masset
Cuisine:	Classic international, regional and original specialties
Price:	$27.50 per person. Includes a five-course dinner, homemade bread, coffee and chocolate. Wine is extra.
Credit Cards:	American Express, MasterCard, Visa
Hours:	Restaurant seating is at 7 p.m. on Thursday and Friday, 6 and 9 p.m. on Saturday. The manor is available for banquets and private parties of 12 or more on days the is not open.
Remarks:	Reservations required.

Birchfield Manor rests on six acres of land and was built in 1910 by Yakima sheep rancher, Thomas Smith. In 1979, Wil and Sandy Masset purchased this 2 1/2-story Victorian-style home. After some minor remodeling, Birchfield Manor opened and began serving its memorable meals to guests.

A long driveway guides you easily to the manor, which is surrounded by lush green grass and trees. The sharp contrast between the manor and the barren desert is startling and beautiful.

A World Class Restaurant

Chef Masset apprenticed at the Olympic Hotel (now the Four Seasons Olympic) in Seattle. He completed his training in Europe at St. Moritz, Switzerland. Chef Wil combines regional specialties with classic, international flare. The result is a wonderful blend of contemporary foods like loin of pork stuffed with Eastern Washington goat cheese, served with hazelnut sauce—all prepared in classic style.

The menus at Birchfield change weekly. Each new menu offers a choice of four entrees. These choices include fresh fish, steak, a chicken or pork dish, and a special chef's selection. Each five-course dinner includes vegetables, manor-baked bread and chocolate. A recent menu offered an appetizer of chicken ravioli Florentine, French-style beef bouillon with leeks and maifun salad. Entree choices included filet of Hawaiian mahi mahi with macadamia nut and lemon butter, tenderloin steak en brochette or Cajun-style sauteed pork tenderloin medallions with Cajun mushrooms and vegetable sauce.

For a sweet ending, Chef Masset imports Callebaut chocolate from Belgium, and makes the delicious truffles served at the end of every meal. He also sculpts chocolate—creating seasonal designs like sleighs and spring baskets.

Fresh is Best

On Thursdays, Chef Masset goes to market to select the finest local meats and produce available. In the spring and summer, Sandy and Wil visit nearby farms to hand-pick the fruits and vegetables Yakima is known for. Fresh herbs grow in the manor's flower beds and Chef Masset's own hot house supplies Birchfield with lettuces, tomatoes, pumpkins and the like.

A Well-stocked Wine Cellar

With close proximity to the many wineries of the Yakima Valley, Birchfield has a wine cellar containing over 400 wines, including wines from Washington, Oregon and California. Tours of the cellar can be arranged upon request.

Getting There

From Yakima, take Interstate 82 south to Exit 34. Take Exit 34 to State Highway 24, eastbound. Travel two miles. Turn right on Birchfield Road. The Manor is the first house on the right.

The restaurant is in a two-and-a-half story home.

brusseau's in edmonds

Address: Fifth and Dayton, Edmonds, WA 98020
Telephone: (206) 774-4166
Host: Jerilyn Brusseau
Cuisine: Northwest regional
Prices: Breakfast $1 to $3.95, lunch $2.90 to $5.75
Credit Cards: MasterCard, Visa
Hours: Monday through Friday 7 a.m. to 6 p.m., Saturday 8 a.m. to 6 p.m., Sunday 8 a.m. to 4 p.m. in winter; one hour later in summer; open for breakfast and lunch only

brusseau's is located in Edmonds, the fashionable town brushing Seattle's northern fringe. It is a daytime place where the early morning air is scented with irresistible aromas from brusseau's own bakery. Local business people know to gather here for morning coffee and the sumptuous selection of baked goods from extra-sour baguettes to pear butter almond swirls. The cafe is also a lunchtime spot where people meet under bright Cinzano umbrellas for a sidewalk picnic, or around cozy tables inside for a warm, leisurely meal. On weekends, brusseau's is a brunch spot.

Country floral wallpaper wraps the dining area in peach and ivory tones that are mirrored in the woven tablecloths.   Local artists' work and grapevine wreaths augment the homey feeling.

Fresh and Local

Jerilyn Brusseau, owner and cook, is acclaimed as one of the Northwest's finest restaurateurs. Devoted to innovative preparation of fresh local foods, Jerilyn's philosophy is to promote the farmer and educate the people about the foods they eat. She works diligently to carry out her beliefs, foraging ingredients from many sources in the Northwest. Local honey, Canadian hard pear and apple cider, fresh wild mushrooms, microbrewery beer, and fresh churned butter are among her finds. Fruits and vegetables are harvested from Northwest farms, and jams and jellies are prepared by Jerilyn's father, Grandpa Cheney. As the menu says, "Everything at brusseau's is created to nourish not only the body but the mind and the spirit as well."

Bakery and More

brusseau's bakery produces a selection of breads (including the popular seven grain nutrient), bagels and rolls. Wild huckleberry lemon rolls and apple carrot banana bran muffins share the bakery case with a selection of cream cheese swirls, buttery croissants and farmhouse cookies. "Chocolate

Decadence" and famous cheesecakes are among the daily dessert selections.

Breakfast specialties include French toast with Vermont maple syrup, ham and cheese croissants, and cream cheese scrambled eggs. Homemade quiches are found on the breakfast and lunch menus. Weekend breakfast is often accompanied by music performed by a local artist.

Lunch entrées and soups change daily, and are listed on a hanging chalkboard. Homemade soups such as "Duchess Vegetarian" warm a wintery day, while fresh salads are favorites any season. Roast turkey salad with hazelnuts, and the Idaho wild and brown rice salad with Oregon shrimp and light herb vinaigrette are among the salad selections.

Jerilyn's son, Jeffrey, and daughter, Mari, join the cheerful, dependable staff and handle brusseau's catering, including weddings, business meetings, picnics and other functions. Just one specialty off the catering menu is a wheel of creamy brie surrounded by a homemade crusty, cracked wheat braid.

Getting There

Head north on I-5 and take the Edmonds-Kingston ferry Exit. Continue west into downtown Edmonds on Fifth Avenue. brusseau's is on the corner of Fifth and Dayton, across from the Old Milltown.

Jerilyn is devoted to preparing fresh local foods in innovative ways.

HOME BY THE SEA

Address:	2388 East Sunlight Beach Road, Clinton, WA 98236
Telephone:	(206) 221-2964
Location:	On the southwest coast of Whidbey Island, six miles from the Clinton ferry
Hosts:	Sharon Fritts-Drew, Helen Fritts, Joyce Fritts Alexander
Room & Cottage Rates:	$90 to $140 double
Credit Cards:	Discover, MasterCard and Visa. Personal and travelers checks preferred.
Remarks:	No pets. Room rates include full breakfast; cottages provided with "Breakfast Baskets" and complete kitchen. Special packages available.

Whidbey Island is the longest island in the contiguous United States, stretching north and south for nearly 50 miles in Washington's Puget Sound. On the southwest corner of the island, tucked under Double Bluff, is Useless Bay. Upon the shore of this wide, shallow bay is the Home by the Sea — Whidbey Island's first bed and breakfast.

Innkeeper Sharon Fritts-Drew has taught in several different countries and traveled in 49. She created the bed and breakfast on the beach where she returned every summer for 20 years; the place where she encourages others to "take a pause from the hurried world." Upon arrival at Home by the Sea, the aroma of candles and cookies permeates the air, and the pace of the city is soon shed. The Fritts-Drew family offers two rooms in the main house. Four additional cottages are located within a five-mile radius. The smorgasbord of choices include the Nordic Cottage on Lone Lake with private fishing dock; Cape Cod Cottage, a 1940s sea coast family accommodation with beach access; and Swiss Chalet and Chanterelle tucked in fir and pine trees for a totally relaxing experience.

At Home

Guest rooms in the Home face west for a view across the bay to the Olympic Mountains. A natural bird sanctuary, this sandy realm is home to eagles, geese, ducks and sandpipers. The "Sunset Room," a queen bed suite, has a private bath. The "Seabreeze" has a double bed and private bath. The latter also offers a sitting room with a single bed. Sharon's multi-cultural accents — an Egyptian camel footstool, a Turkish brass urn, and a collection of beaded purses — grace each room. In the closets hang plush bathrobes for your excursion to the hot tub, which is on a deck near the beach.

The living room, with its broad picture windows facing the bay, is furnished with Persian carpets and Middle Eastern treasures. Breakfast is served in the neighboring dining room with the same spectacular view. Standard morning fare is eggs Benedict, crepes or soufflé, accompanied by homemade muffins and breads, juice, fresh fruit and brewed coffee or tea.

Not Inn

Home by the Sea's four cottages offer the ultimate in atmosphere and seclusion. Each has a fully equipped kitchen stocked with a special "Breakfast Basket." Tables are pre-set with elegant china, and guests may rise at their leisure to prepare breakfast. Wood and kindling are provided for each place. The cottages have minimum stay requirements on the weekends, so it is best to check with Sharon when making reservations.

Just down the road from the Home, the 1940s Cape Cod Cottage serves as a perfect family retreat with two double beds, a child's single and a crib. The natural cedar interior is accented by a Kabul camel blanket, antique furniture and a brick fireplace. A picnic table and barbeque are found in the backyard, which overlooks Deer Lagoon.

The Nordic Cottage, three miles from the Fritts-Drew home, overlooks quiet Lone Lake. A private dock floats in the lily pads, and the lake is known for excellent trout fishing in summer and ice-skating in winter. Its wood-burning stove, Danish lace curtains, hardwood floors, and Norwegian treasures create a romantic getaway. The cozy bedroom features a Queen bed and a lake view. A large, open kitchen with butcher block counters and a dishwasher make food preparation easy.

Sequestered in a deep forest, just five miles from the Home by the Sea, are two charming cottages: the Swiss Chalet and the Chanterelle. The Hansel and Gretel style Swiss Chalet is decorated with floral print wallpaper and French lace. Upstairs, an Eiderdown covers each double bed. The beds are romantically located under a skylighted ceiling. Nearby, on the same two acres of fir and pine, is the Chanterelle Cottage. A brick planter and flower trellis brighten the outside with a glider swing in a forest setting. Lace pillow slips accent the cottage's double bed. Prints from Morrocco and Spain are displayed on the living room walls, and a wood burning stove warms the room.

Out and About

Nearby Merkerk Rhododendron Gardens is a special treat for flower lovers. From March through May, grand bushes reaching 25 feet in height display brilliant flowers of all shades. Coupeville, located mid-island on Penn Cove, is one of the oldest towns in the state. It features Victorian homes, an 1855 blockhouse, and specialty shops and restaurants.

The separate Swiss Chalet sits alone in acres of trees.

Whidbey is an island of pasture land, farms and barns. A drive along its winding roads will lead you through rural communities to the Greenbank Berry Farm, the largest loganberry field in the world. Tours are available, as well as a tasting room for Chateau Ste. Michelle wines.

Getting There

Home by the Sea is reached by driving north on I-5 from Seattle to the Mukilteo—Clinton ferry, Exit 189 (eleven miles). Drive four miles to the ferry landing and board the Washington State ferry for a 15-minute ride. Drive on Highway 525 north for six miles to Bayview center. Turn left on Howard Road and left again on Bayview Road. Continue one mile to Sunlight Beach Road and turn right. Please be extra cautious when driving down this narrow beach road. There are often children at play. Continue to the end of the road; the inn is on the left.

INN AT LANGLEY

Address:	P.O. Box 835, 400 First Street, Langley, WA 98260
Telephone:	(206) 221-3033
Location:	Whidbey Island, on Saratoga Passage
Hosts:	Sandra and Steve Nogal
Room Rates:	$95 guest room; $110 corner guest room; $175 suite
Credit Cards:	American Express, MasterCard, Visa
Remarks:	Rates include buffet breakfast.

Perched on an edge of land, just above Saratoga Passage in Puget Sound, sits the Inn at Langley. An adult retreat of the highest caliber, the Inn offers an ideal location for a romantic weekend, a corporate gathering or a time of solitude.

The inn's 24 rooms are separate enough to ensure privacy, but they lend a sense of being part of a greater entity. There is a world of wildlife that shares the environment. Whales swim the passage, eagles soar in the sky, heron stalk the marshes. The peace of the island is gentle and renewing.

The newly opened inn combines elements of the natural Northwest with the understatement of Asian design. The colors of the beach and the feel of the forest have been brought indoors, creating harmony between the interior and the outdoors. Peeled pine poles accent sand-colored walls. Nubby, neutral carpeting simulate Japanese woven mats. Private decks with upholstered benches overlook the water and are accented with colorful flowers and shrubs.

The innkeepers, Sandra and Steve Nogal, are ever-present and attentive to the needs of their guests. With several year's experience in the hospitality industry, the couple is well-equipped to handle the details of operating the inn. "We want to share this quietly rich place with you," says Sandy. Their careful attention is evident in the list of amenities. Each room contains a wood-burning fireplace. Televisions, refrigerators, and coffee percolators are standard features. Spacious bathrooms have large showers and over-sized jacuzzis that face the sea and the fire. Plush towels and hotel-monogrammed terry robes are provided for guests to use.

All rooms have spectacular views—at least 180 degrees. The six corner rooms have even more expansive views because of the extra windows. Two suites offer separate sleeping arrangements and a sofa-bed in the living room. Two of the four floors are wheelchair accessible.

The Inn at Langley has a conference room that accommodates 25 to 30 people board-room style. Eighteen-foot ceilings and a view of the passage help create a relaxed setting. Audio-visual equipment is available, including an electronic projection screen.

The inn's environs are a blend of Northwest woods and edible gardens. Lanky vine maples stretch skyward in lightwells. Fruit trees and berry bushes flank the grounds. On the street level, a Japanese-style waterfall flows quietly over two tiers of rock.

Country Kitchen

The large country kitchen adjoins the dining room. From this open kitchen, Innkeeper/chef Steve produces an abundance of good food. A drop-in buffet breakfast is offered to all guests. Steve's freshly-baked muffins and Danish accompany the inn's favorite granola and fruit.

Diners can congregate around the long Frank Lloyd Wright-designed cherry table for lively conversation, or one of the smaller tables lining the room. A river-rock fireplace dominates this dining room which overlooks the water.

Steve serves dinner Friday and Saturday nights. This prix fixe meal features Northwest ingredients such as salt marsh lamb, forest morels, winter blackmouth salmon, and fresh loganberries. "We try to use local ingredients that reflect the island's offerings," says Steve. He is happy to share his recipes with the guests.

The inn's wine cellar is built into the foundation of the kitchen. Focusing on wines from the Northwest, the 3,500-bottle cellar also includes selections from California, Europe and Australia. Wines can be ordered to accompany dinner service or for room service.

Island Exploration

Primarily rural, Whidbey Island deserves investigation. And Langley is a good place to start. Langley is a casual seaside village with a turn-of-the-century feel. Unique shops feature local art and handiwork. Antiques, gifts and books are purveyed in the small, sophisticated stores. A half dozen restaurants are within walking distance of the inn, featuring cuisine from Mediterranean to Mexican. For a bit of local flavor, drop into the Doghouse Tavern for a beer. Grocery and liquor stores are also close by.

Guests who enjoy outdoor activities can choose to bike, kayak, fish or windsurf. Golf enthusiasts might wish to try the Island Greens course in Clinton. This Scottish-style course offers well-maintained turf that uses a minimum amount of pesticides.

All of the rooms face the water.

At Greenbank, Ste. Michelle Winery maintains the Whidbey's Liqueur distillery and a tasting room. Sample this unique beverage made from local loganberries. The winery offers other products as well.

Steve and Sandy have discovered the best places for watching sunsets no matter what the season. They will gladly share their secrets, and even suggest a few picnic spots.

Getting There

From Seattle, take I-5 north to Exit 189 (Whidbey Island-Mukilteo Ferry), following signs to ferry landing. Boats depart every half-hour. Arriving Clinton, follow State Highway 525 north to Maxwelton Road. Turn right. Proceed to the end of the road. Bear left onto Langley Road. Continue on to Cascade, which becomes First Street. The inn is on the right.

SARATOGA INN

Address:	4850 South Coles Road, Langley, Whidbey Island, WA 98260
Telephone:	(206) 221-7526
Location:	On the southeastern side of Whidbey Island, 10 minutes from the Mukilteo-Columbia Beach ferry landing.
Host:	Debbie Jones, innkeeper
Room Rates:	$80 to $95, including breakfast
Credit Cards:	None.
Remarks:	No smoking, no children, no pets.

This lovely two-story home atop a hill overlooking Saratoga Passage is more like a country estate than a typical bed and breakfast inn. Standing on 25 acres, it has splendid views of Saratoga Passage, Camano Island, the Cascade Mountains, especially Mount Baker. You enter through a picket fence to a lovely old-fashioned English cottage garden, laced with brick paths and planted in phlox, peonies, black-eyed susans and Queen Anne's lace.

The shingle-clad inn was built in 1982 and has such fine details as sunburst gables, beveled-glass windows, hardwood floors and a used-brick fireplace to provide the warmth and tradition of a country home.

Distinctive Bedrooms

Five large bedrooms, each with a private bath, are located on the second floor. The Willow room has a Franklin stove, bent willow bed and rocker, and a used-brick hearth. The bedroom has splendid views to the north and east of the mountains, Saratoga Passage, meadows and gardens. The Country Garden room is a good spot for watching ships or storms next to another cozy Franklin stove. It's furnished with an iron and brass bed. Queen Anne's Lace has twin beds and the best view of Camano Head rising from Puget Sound, with the snow-capped Cascades in the distance. A peeled pine headboard, chair and rocker add a country flavor to the Meadow room, which faces southwest to catch the sunset. The Hollyhock room overlooks meadow and forest and is furnished with an old pine door for a headboard and a nautical deck chair that is ideal for relaxing.

The living room is dominated by a big fireplace and furnished with country antiques, Chippendale and Queen Anne furniture. There are books and board games for guests to enjoy.

Extra Touches

The inn's extra touches reflect the care and hard work of Debbie Jones. Her children grown and gone she loves meeting her guests at the door and welcoming them to her Inn. She places fresh flowers in the rooms and includes scented soaps and down pillows. Quilts that she made decorate several rooms. Her attention to detail extends to the needlework luggage rack straps she made to match the sheets.

Guests can help themselves to breakfast between 8:30 and 9. The meal includes freshly ground coffee, croissants, blueberry muffins, homemade blackberry jam, fruit compote, applesauce or rhubarb from the garden and can be eaten on the deck, which has fine views of the water and mountains. There is a treehouse that sees plenty of adult time for afternoon tea or cocktails.

An Island for Bicycling

The normally quiet Whidbey Island roads are ideal for bicycling. Whidbey, the longest island in the United States and is well suited to leisurely exploring, either by bicycle or by car. Mostly rural, the island is covered with a network of roads that takes you past peaceful pasturelands, by pioneering homesteads and down to secluded coves and beaches. Like the San Juan Islands, traffic is largely a matter of waves of cars just before or after a ferry has docked. The rest of the time the roads are only lightly used.

Exploring Whidbey Island

As you'd expect, the island gets plenty of summer visitors, but if you want to savor the peace and quiet, drink in the splendid views of the mountains and the sound and poke around the nooks and crannies at your own pace, go in spring, fall or winter.

In the spring, yellow scotch broom, lilacs and the showy white blossoms of red-berry elder and madrona brighten the roadsides. In May, the island's native rhododendrons burst into pink bloom. Fall and winter are great for watching migratory waterfowl head south. Winter is also a time for storm-watching, either on Whidbey's beaches or tucked away in this warm and comfortable bed and breakfast inn.

Langley, the nearest settlement to the Saratoga Inn, is a compact little town with neat, trim houses, a white-steepled church and a main street that is positioned on a bluff overlooking Saratoga Passage. The shopping is good, especially if you like to search out antiques.

If you're a history buff, Fort Casey State Park, adjacent to the Keystone-Port Townsend ferry dock, is a real treasure. Built at the turn of the century, it was one of the three coast artillery forts that guarded the entrance to Admiralty Inlet

Books and board games are available.

against flotillas of dreadnoughts that never materialized. The old casements and magazines are fascinating. The huge "disappearing" 10-inch coastal guns are not the originals; they were retrieved from similar forts in the Philippines several years ago. The lighthouse contains a small museum describing the fort.

Coupeville is one of the oldest towns in the state and retains many buildings dating from the second half of the 19th century. Most of them bear plaques giving the buildings' names and years of construction.

Getting There

From Seattle, take I-5 north to the Whidbey Island-Mukilteo Ferry exit 189 (eleven miles) and proceed to the ferry landing (four miles). The ferry to Clinton is a 15-minute ride. Follow Highway 525 north toward Langley and turn right on Langley Road. The Saratoga Inn is located at the intersection of Coles Road and Brooks Hill Road.

TURTLEBACK FARM INN

Address: Route 1, P.O. Box 650, Eastsound, WA 98245
Telephone: (206) 376-4914
Location: Six miles from Orcas Island ferry landing in Crow Valley
Hosts: Bill and Susan Fletcher, Innkeepers
Room Rates: $65 to $135
Credit Cards: MasterCard, Visa
Remarks: No smoking inside, no pets, no infants. Children by special arrangement.

Turtleback Mountain swells up from the west lobe of Orcas Island, one of nearly 172 islands in Washington State's San Juan Archipelago. The island's rim is 125 miles of arythmic coastline. Its interior is a collage of valleys, ponds and meadows. Upon one of these meadows, submerged in tranquility, rests the Turtleback Farm Inn.

This restored 100-year-old farmhouse has all the charm of a country manor. The setting is serene, complete with grasslands, barns and outbuildings, 300-year-old maples and a pond well stocked with trout (catch and release). Turtleback Farm Inn, completely renovated by the Fletchers in 1985, combines country farmhouse living with a comfortable guest retreat.

Hanging on the wall inside the front door is an ad from the September 22, 1933, Seattle Daily Times, featuring the film *Tarzan the Fearless*. The ad reads, "Buster Crabbe, muscular Olympic swimming champion, whose latest screen appearance brings excitement aplenty to the Roxy Theater." The famous actor is Susan's father.

A Touch of Class

Each of Turtleback's seven individually decorated guest rooms reflect the Fletchers' careful attention to detail. All are unique, from the "Meadow Room" with its expansive view to the "Nook," which is reminiscent of a ship's cabin. Spotless Northwest fir floors throughout the inn are softened by imported rugs. French floral print cottons envelope woolly comforters — some of the wool is directly from the backs of the sheep grazing outside. The living room is a cozy gathering place for inn guests.

Fresh Start

Dining room tables are set with stark white linens, fine china and silver, and a turtle-shaped trivet with a pot of freshly ground coffee or brewed tea. Fresh juice and fruits begin the meal. During the summer there are fresh berries from

the island; the fall brings apples from the trees right on the farm. Next comes Susan's famed granola. (She'll proudly share the recipe.) As diners crunch along, Susan is busy preparing the next course, which may be an omelette served with muffins or homemade bread, or perhaps a corn waffle accompanied by sausage or bacon. Celtic harp music wafts in from the kitchen as guests begin their Orcas day in fine fashion.

An Orcas For Everyone

Trails descend from Turtleback Farm Inn into the meadows below. Domestic chickens, ducks and geese share the land with several varieties of migratory birds. The forests, pastures and meadows are home to the farm's flock of sheep and grazing charlois cattle.

A visitor to Orcas will not leave Turtleback Inn without a map of the island, complete with Fletchers' heiroglyphics denoting points of interest, as well as some personal advise on what to see and do. As Bill says, "These are some of the richest waters I've seen." Fishing is always a favorite sport as Orcas' waters are an obliging host to salmon and cod. Bicycling, sailing, canoeing and kayaking are common island activities. A walk along the beach at Obstruction Pass is a prime way to view sea lions and perhaps the dorsal fin of an Orca whale disappearing into the sound—there are 88 resident Orcas who pass by regularly.

Cascade Lake at Moran State Park is a wonderful place to stretch out after a long sleep at Turtleback. In addition to swimming, the lake offers bass and trout fishing from small rental boats, or a chance to try out the paddle boats.

Hikers will enjoy circumnavigating Cascade Lake, or one of the many other trails in Moran State Park. An easy quarter-mile walk through the forest brings hikers to Rustic and Cascade Falls. For the more ambitious, Mt. Constitution awaits — its 2,409 feet creates a challenging hike to the highest point in the San Juan archipelago, but the view is well worth the effort. For those with ease in mind, you can drive to the top and limit your hiking to the stairs of the monument at the summit.

Explore in the Off-Season

Midweek and off-season visitors will be rewarded with the added serenity and true flavor of the island. Crowds are down, the pace is slower, so there is simply more of the island's charm just for you. Fall colors brighten the landscape, and spring brings the pastels of flowering plants and trees. Winter comes with its own mood, complete with storms and misty nights.

Returning to the Turtleback Farm Inn's welcoming fire is a fine way to end the day. Guests are invited to use the wet bar, which is always stocked with special teas, coffees and cocoa. There is also a decanter of sherry on a nearby cart.

Rooms in the 100-year old farmhouse overlook the original homestead.

Bill and Susan live in a separate home on the farm, so in the evening when they retire to their home, guests can experience having the entire farmhouse to themselves. This is an ideal situation if you come up with your own group during the off-season and occupy the entire inn. The seclusion of the inn has proven to be an ideal atmosphere for small meetings and planning sessions.

Getting There

Orcas Island may be reached by a float plane service from Seattle International Airport or downtown Seattle. You may take the Washington state ferry from Anacortes with you car or as a walk-on passenger. From Seattle take I-5 north and follow the signs to the Anacortes ferry landing. Upon arrival on Orcas, drive two and one-half miles on Horseshoe Highway. Turn left at the road sign which indicates Turtleback Farm Inn. Travel one mile and turn right on Crow Valley. Continue two and four-tenths miles to the inn.

CHRISTINA'S

Address:	Main Street, Eastsound, WA 98245
Telephone:	(206) 376-4904
Location:	On Main Street in Eastsound, Orcas Island
Host:	Christina Gentry
Cuisine:	Natural Northwest
Prices:	12.50 to $17.50
Credit Cards:	American Express, Carte Blanche, Diner's Club, MasterCard, Visa
Hours:	6 p.m. to midnight daily June 12 to August 15. 5 p.m. to 10 p.m. Thursday through Monday the rest of the year. Brunch served Sunday from 9:30 a.m. Closed New Year's Day to Valentine's Day.

This little hamlet on the shore of Orcas Island's Eastsound Bay seems an unlikely spot for one of the state's top-rated restaurants. Eastsound's Main Street runs little more than four blocks and houses only a single structure taller than one story. That building is the Island Union Building, and its second story contains Christina's, a cozy restaurant with a broad view of the the bay.

Orcas Island is but one in the chain of 172 San Juan islands. One of the largest islands, it sports a year-round population of nearly 1,500. Eastsound is the hub of culture and cuisine. Both visitors and locals alike recognize Christina's as "the" restaurant on the island.

Natural Northwest Cuisine

Christina Gentry selects and prepares the meals herself. Fresh, locally grown products include seafood from the cold waters of Puget Sound, oysters from the island, mussels from nearby Lopez Island, poultry and lamb from Lopez.

All meals are prepared with simplicity and distinction. Few sauces, if any, are used in most dishes, reflecting Christina's stong belief that the natural flavors of the food should remain pure. "This is what I call natural Northwest cooking," she says. "I want to serve only fresh local products as simply and purely as is possible." For instance, the restaurant's generous serving of poached salmon is glazed with basil, then served with a fresh garden salad, fresh vegetables and just-picked new potatoes.

The menus change with the season and the readiness of the natural ingredients. The poultry may be pheasant, game hen or chicken. The meat may be a different cut each evening. A specialty is the rich Christina's bouillabaisse, lavishly packed with fresh, local shellfish and served with one of the 50 or 60 regional wines stocked by Christina.

Christina's desserts bring back the meaning to after-dinner treats. She serves fresh berry tarts, or homemade ice cream, such as lavender honey and espresso, homemade piña colada cheesecake.

A former art student, Christina takes pride in her collection of Oriental rugs, copperware and old kitchen implements almost as much as she does her culinary skills.

The restaurant is a blend of both talents. Each table has a direct view of the bay; the blue tablecloths capture and extend the colors of the sea. Fresh flowers and chic china add elegance to the setting. Oil lamps provide soft light, blending with the setting sun.

There is a marvelous postage-stamp-size lounge off of the dining room for dining, or relaxing over a drink before or after the meal.

Getting There

In Eastsound, the two-story Island Union Building on Main Street is easily recognizable; turn into the adjacent alley and walk up the stairs.

The seafood comes from the local waters.

THE INN AT SEMIAHMOO

Address:	9565 Semiahmoo Parkway, Blaine WA 98230
Telephone:	In Washington (206) 371-2000. Nationwide (800) 854-2608. In Canada (800) 854-6742.
Host:	Brian Peterson, Director of Marketing
Rates:	November through February: $90 to $150 single or double. From March through April: $105 to $155. May through October $125 to $190. Executive suites are available.
Cuisine:	Contemporary Northwest
Credit Cards:	American Express, Diners Club, MasterCard, Visa
Remarks:	Reservations recommended.

Semi-ah-moo is a Salish Indian name for "half moon bay." The Indians who inhabited the area long ago probably named it that because of the beautiful golden moon that seems to dip halfway below the horizon into the bay. The Inn at Semiahmoo rests on the tip of a natural sandspit that juts out into the water, and is surrounded by some of the most beautiful country found in the Pacific Northwest. The Canadian border is to the north, Mt. Baker is East, Vancouver Island is west and to the South are the beautiful San Juan Islands.

Some History

In 1894, the Alaska Packers Association of San Francisco started the APA salmon cannery on the site where the inn is now. It was considered a showpiece cannery. In 1916, it was sold to Del Monte of California and salmon continued to be packed there until 1964. With the construction starting in 1985, Atlas Hotels of San Diego renovated and incorporated many of the original cannery structures into the building design. The Inn at Semiahmoo opened for business in June of 1987.

Warmth and Charm

Six miles of gently curving road travels through a wooded resort community to Semiahmoo. The inn is a graceful four-story, L-shaped structure. A wide drive leads to the lobby entrance. Just inside is a large fireplace made from original cannery brick. The floors and much of the walls and woodwork are light buttery fir and hemlock, both indigenous to the area. High ceilings, lots of windows, green plants and gleaming brass create an elegant warm atmosphere even on a rare gray day.

Panoramic Splendor

Semiahmoo was built to take advantage of views of the surrounding water. Almost all 200 guest rooms enjoy a spectacular view. The rooms are large. Many have fireplaces. Some even have skylights. Light pine, dark teal carpeting, and softly colored wallpaper continue the warm, elegant atmosphere found throughout the hotel.

Divine Dining

Stars, named after the first ship commissioned to the Alaska Packers Association, is the hotel's main restaurant. It serves breakfast, lunch and dinner. The restaurant is elegant and intimate. White linen, china and silver adorn every table. The restaurant's wine list is extensive with wines from Washington, Oregon, California and France. All menus at Stars offer special entrees made with less salt and cholesterol for guests on restricted diets.

The R and R, or Research Restaurant, is a second dining facility, that is researching both a name and a menu based on comments from the guests. It is a moderately priced steak and salmon house. The atmosphere is casual.

Packer's Lounge is located in the original "pack house" where salmon were sorted and canned. Large windows take advantage of the ocean view in this elegant yet relaxed lounge. Leather bar stools and wicker chairs mix comfortably around a dark green marble bar and tables. Live entertainment provides the opportunity to dance the night away. The oyster bar, just off Packer's Lounge, is a great place to grab a quick bite before going off sightseeing.

Take a Cruise

Get aboard the 80-foot *Star of Semiahmoo*. This ship can carry up to 300 passengers. It has a sound system covering both decks and a food and beverage service. Seals, eagles and even Orca whales can be viewed during the four-hour cruise. Binoculars are provided for each passenger. The *Star of Semiahmoo* also has a sunset cruise. Relax, be romantic and watch the sun go down from the decks of this intimate cruise vessel.

The *Emerald Star* sportfishing cruiser departs daily for Boundary Bay and the Strait of Georgia. Fish for lingcod, rockfish, halibut and salmon. The trip includes bait, tackle and fish-cleaning. A complementary return trip is offered to anyone who doesn't catch a fish.

For Land Lovers

Semiahmoo is the place for a great game of golf. The 18-hole course was designed by Arnold Palmer and in its first full year of operation was named "the best new resort golf course in the USA" by *Golf Digest*. The fairways were

Packer's Lounge is where salmon were once canned.

carved out of natural forest. Penncross Bent grass covers both the fairways and the greens. Four lakes and 54 sand traps keep the game challenging. Guests of the inn can reserve tee times when they make room reservations.

Keep Fit, Have Fun

The health center at Semiahmoo offers a variety of fitness and recreational activities. It is staffed by pros including a licensed aerobics instructor. The center includes a 10-station Universal gym, Life cycles and rowing machines. Try out the jogging tracks or challenge a pal to tennis, squash or racquetball. For a grand finale, enjoy a sauna, steam or swim in the pool.

Getting There

From I-5 north or southbound, take Exit 270 (Birch Bay-Lynden). Follow the signs (approximately six and three-tenths miles) to the Inn at Semiahmoo.

Western Canada

In our travels throughout Western Canada, Mardi and I have been struck by its raw, muscular beauty. Its population centers heavily around a few urban areas, Victoria and Vancouver, Calgary and Edmonton, leaving the rest sparsely developed and scenically spectacular. From the jagged fjord-carved coast of Vancouver Island to the long, glittering inland lakes of Alberta, we've seen diverse and unparalleled beauty. Mystical islands, ice-chiseled mountain ranges, tropical hot springs and rolling range lands are all a part of Western Canada's mosaic.

The nine thousand years of native cultural history is as fascinating as its physical setting is dramatic. Intrepid coastal peoples congregated where fish were plentiful. Inland tribes were generally nomadic and depended on hunting for survival. Today, these people are famous for their high quality crafts, masks and totem poles, weavings and ceremonial regalia — all testimony to a skilled and highly developed ancestry. Ancient petroglyphs, or rock carvings, are among the cultural legacies left by these peoples. The days of potlatches, tribal wars and cedar longhouses are all a part of the cultural fabric, as are the myths, legends and beliefs of the native Canadians. One of the most comprehensive collection of artifacts to be found is in Victoria's Provincial Museum.

Today's largest group of inhabitants are the descendants of English, Scottish, Irish and Welsh immigrants. Canadians are warm and hospitable people, perhaps more polite and conversive than Americans. A close community spirit prevails even in the larger cities, making travel easy and enjoyable.

Travel Tips for Western Canada

Canada operates on the metric system. A few simple and easy to remember guidelines are as follows:

Distances and speed limits are posted in kilometers. To convert kilometers to miles, drop the last digit and multiply by six. To convert miles to kilometers, multiply by 1.6. Thus, 100 km/hr = 10 x 6 = 60 mi/hr. Gasoline is measured in liters. One liter equals .26 gallons, one gallon equals 3.79 liters.

Temperatures are measured on the Celsius scale. To convert Celsius to Fahrenheit, multiply by nine-fifths and add 32. To convert from Fahrenheit to Celsius, subtract 32 and multiply by five-ninths.

The provinces require visiting motorists to produce evidence of financial responsibility if involved in an accident. The use of seat belts is compulsory.

Visitors are urged to exchange currency after arrival. Normal banking hours are 10 a.m. to 3 p.m. Monday through Friday. Most shops and businesses will accept U.S. dollars, but will most likely offer a lower exchange rate.

Major American bank and credit cards are honored in Canada. Purchases are billed at the U.S. dollar equivalent of the Canadian price.

Customs and Border Crossings

All visitors must clear Canadian customs when entering Canada and when returning to the United States. It is a simple procedure, yet there are a few regulations. Border traffic tends to be heavier on weekends, particularly Sunday nights, so plan accordingly. Passports are not necessary for U.S. citizens; however, proof of citizenship is required. If you are bringing dogs or cats over three months old, you must have a certificate of rabies vaccination within the past 36 months. Canadian customs regulations permit you to bring personal baggage, recreational equipment, two days' food supply and your vehicle. All non-consumable items must leave the country with you.

When reentering the United States, you may bring back $400 (U.S. dollars) worth of duty-free articles for personal or household use or as gifts, if you have been out of the country for at least 48 hours. Additionally, you must not have claimed the exemption in the past 30 days. You may include for exemption 100 cigars and 200 cigarettes, and one liter of wine, beer or liquor. Your exemption is $25 (U.S. dollars) if you have been gone less than 48 hours or have claimed the $400 exemption within the past 30 days. You may include 50 cigarettes, 10 cigars, five ounces of alcoholic beverages, and five ounces of perfume containing alcohol or proportionate amounts of each. When entering the U.S., you must declare, at the price paid, everything acquired in Canada that you are taking home, including gifts given to you and articles worn or used. Penalties apply for failure to declare. Direct specific customs inquiries to: Revenue Customs, Customs and Excise, Public Relations Branch, Ottawa, Ontario, Canada, K1A 0L5 (613) 993-6220.

Liquor Laws

The minimum drinking age in Alberta is 18 and 19 in British Columbia. All alcoholic beverages by the bottle (including wine and beer) are sold in provincial liquor stores. Penalties are stiff for drinking and driving, and are strictly enforced. It is a criminal offense for a driver to refuse to provide a breath or blood sample when required by a Peace Officer.

Information Sources for Western Canada

Minister of Tourism and Provincial Secretary
Parliament Buildings
Victoria, B.C. Canada V8V 1X4
(800) 663-6000

Travel Alberta
15th Floor
10025 Jasper Ave.
Edmonton, Alberta T5J3
(800) 661-8888

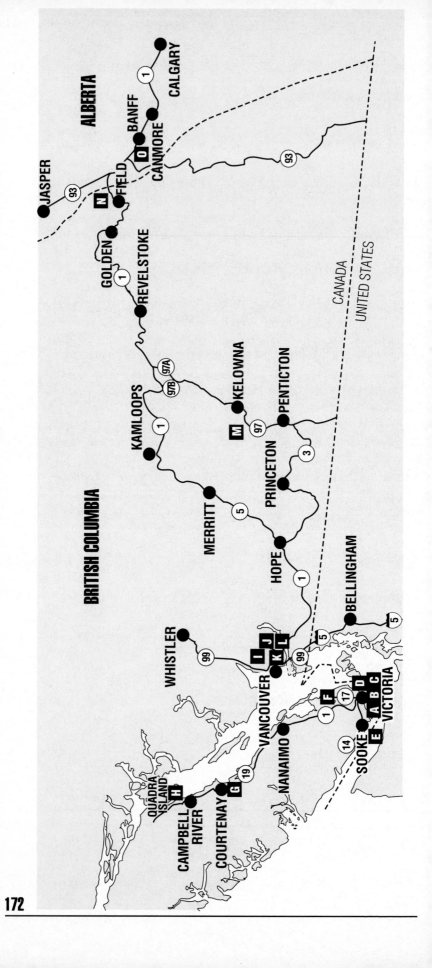

WESTERN CANADA SPECIAL PLACES

A   The Bedford Hotel

B   Abigail's Hotel

C   The Beaconsfield Inn

D   Chez Daniel

E   Sooke Harbour House

F   Hastings House

G   The Old House

H   April Point Lodge

I   Park Royal Hotel

J   Corsi Trattoria

K   Bishop's

L   The William Tell

M   Hatheume Lake Lodge

N   Emerald Lake Lodge

O   Buffalo Mountain Lodge

THE BEDFORD HOTEL

Address:	1140 Government Street, Victoria, B.C., V8W 1Y2
Telephone:	(604) 384-6835 or 1-800-661-9255 (in western Canada and U.S.A.)
Location:	Near Victoria's Inner Harbour in Old Town
Host:	Robert Lauzon, General Manager
Room Rates:	May-October: Deluxe room $120; deluxe room with fireplace $170. November-May: Deluxe room $95; deluxe room with fireplace $135. Additional person $25. (Canadian)
Credit Cards:	American Express, MasterCard, Visa
Remarks:	Rates include breakfast and afternoon tea.

Few hotels are able to meet the needs of both the vacationer and the business traveler as thoroughly as Victoria's Bedford, the "elegant small hotel." The Bedford, located in the heart of the shopping and financial district, offers just 40 rooms. Yet, the Bedford provides all the amenities of a much larger hotel and a professional staff dedicated to personal service.

Turn-of-the-Century Elegance

Spanning four floors, the hotel rooms are spacious and comfortable. Each room is unique. Several offering views of Victoria's Inner Harbour or Government Street. The Bedford, built in the early 1900s, reflects turn-of-the-century elegance, with an updated sense of comfort. Custom furnishings, including massive armoirs, corner bookshelves and working desks, grace each room. Special attention is paid to every detail: polished brass door pulls and fixtures, oversized towels, and delicately scented amenities are but a few of the thoughtful touches. Goose-down comforters drape each queen-sized bed, carefully turned-down by hotel staff in the evening.

Sixteen of the Bedford's rooms have jacuzzi tubs; a dozen have natural wood-burning fireplaces. Wet bars in the rooms provide a full selection of soft-drinks and liquors. In keeping with the hotel's uncommon service, a complimentary thermos of steaming coffee can be delivered each morning upon request, hung surreptitiously outside the door in a quilted cozy. Overnight shoe shine and complete valet service are also available.

"We offer the thoughtful services you'd expect from a bed and breakfast, yet we're really a small hotel." says General Manager Robert Lauzon. With a dedication to personal service, Lauzon himself is often seen at the front desk, pouring coffee in the restaurant, or carrying bags for the guests.

Full Service Restaurant

The Bedford maintains a full-service restaurant—The Terrace Dining Room and Lounge—open to both hotel guests and the public. A scrumptous breakfast buffet, served from 7 to 10 a.m., is included in the room rate. Freshly baked muffins, croissants, scones and a selection of fruit juices is available. Specially blended granola is accompanied by yogurt or milk. A daily egg dish, quiche or omelettes, complete the meal.

In addition to the full breakfast, Bedford's guests are invited for complimentary afternoon tea. The Light Tea consists of scones, English sherry trifle and tea or coffee. Traditional Tea is available to the public and augments the Light Tea with finger sandwiches, fruit and crumpets.

The Terrace offers full lunch and dinner service in a quiet, unstuffy atmosphere. The lunch menu features a wide selection of soups, full-meal salads, sandwiches, egg creations and entrees such as Steak and Kidney Pie.

Dinner menus in The Terrace change daily to reflect seasonal availability and fresh ingredients. Fish, poultry and meat entrees are expertly prepared, often with delicate sauces. A substantial wine list is available to complement any meal. The Terrace Lounge is adjacent to the dining room.

Corporate travelers may arrange for catered meals. Banquet and meeting facilities are available for parties from 36 to 100.

The latest addition to the Bedford is the Garrick's Head Pub, located just off the lobby (but with its own entrance from the street to preserve guests' privacy.) Located in the exact spot of the former Garrick's Head Saloon, one of Victoria's original saloons, the pub reflects a bit of history. Quaint and intimate, it features a broad selection of light and dark beers and traditional pub fare. Nightly piano music creates a relaxed atmosphere.

Prime Location

The Bedford is favorably located in the core of Victoria's shopping district and just a short distance from the Parliament buildings and downtown corporate offices. The new Eaton's Mall is just across the street with four floors of department stores and shops—140 in all. Small boutiques and gift shops line Government street, including some of the finest clothiers in Victoria.

The Maritime Museum, in Bastion Square, is housed in the original Provincial Court building. Telling of British Columbia's fascinating maritime history, the museum contains two famous vessels, the *Tilikum*, a 38-foot dugout canoe sailed by Captain Voss from Victoria to England, and *Trekka,* a 20-foot ketch sailed single-handed around the world by John Guzzwell.

Each room has a goose-down comforter covering the queen size bed.

Chinatown is a small area withing walking distance of the Bedford. Fantan Alley, once notorious for its opium dens and gambling houses, now invites exploration. On the corner of Figard and Government rises the "Gate of Harmonius Interest."

Market Square is around the corner from the hotel on Johnson Street. Once a thriving area for businesses catering to whalers and gold-seekers, it now houses an array of shops, restaurants and the occasional street musican.

Getting There

If arriving via vessel into the Inner Harbour, the Bedford may be reached by a short taxi ride. If arriving via the B.C. ferries to Sydney, follow the highway all the way into downtown Victoria. Turn right onto Broughton. Turn right again on Government Street. A temporary loading zone allows check-in to the hotel. Parking is available behind the hotel.

ABIGAIL'S HOTEL

Address:	906 McClure Street, Victora, B.C. V8V 3E7
Telephone:	(604) 388-5363
Location:	A few blocks from the heart of Victoria
Host:	Catherine Wollner, Innkeeper
Room Rates:	$90 to $175 (Canadian), double occupancy. Additional person $22 (Canadian) $85 to $150 (U.S.)
Credit Cards:	MasterCard, Visa
Remarks:	No pets. Rates include breakfast.

"My guideline for the design of Abigail's was 'timeless,'" says owner Bill McKechnie. "I kept thinking 'fanciful,' 'feminine' and 'timeless.'" Abigail's Hotel is a romantic inn set near Victoria's center. Rebuilt from a Tudor apartment building in 1985, it is reminiscent of a European style hotel. Vibrant pansies in carefully aligned beds and forest green and burnt orange trim set against a stucco exterior create a collage of appealing colors and textures. A copy of a Rodin sculpture of a young woman wearing a straw hat festooned with flowers rests on a table inside the front door. "This sculpture," Bill says, "was the influence for Abigail's theme."

Unique Perspectives

Abigail's interior is a geometric masterpiece. Angled archways and vaulted ceilings create unique perspectives on the traditional Tudor design. Surprise nooks, notches and crannies add a humorous touch and evoke a childlike sense of discovery. Soft peach, rose, teal and ivory tones are used throughout the inn, tastefully woven into a homey quilt of color.

Abigail's hotel is set on a quiet residential cul-de-sac. Its four stories offer a broad selection of secluded rooms. Of the 16 rooms, ten feature fireplaces. In two of these, the fireplace is glass enclosed and adjoins the bathroom and living area. Guests may recline in the jacuzzi while viewing the fire. Abigail's service-minded staff keeps rooms stocked with wood so that even third floor residents can easily light a fire on chilly evenings.

Eight guest rooms offer these private bubbling baths, complete with fluffy terry-toweled pillows for total relaxation. The spacious tiled bathrooms are appointed with pedestal sinks and brass fixtures. Glittering crystal chandeliers, eyelet curtains and antiques grace each room. Goose down comforters accent the comfortable beds, four of which are canopied. Four rooms have refrigerators, and several feature pass-throughs by which breakfast may be

discreetly delivered without disrupting guests' privacy. There are no televisions or telephones in the rooms. However, a pay phone is located by the front desk for guests' use.

The library is the primary gathering place for the inn's guests. Stately burgundy couches center around the fireplace. The walls are lined with leather bound volumes. A social hour with wine and imported cheeses takes place in this room on weekends; it is the ideal spot for receptions and weddings.

Abigail's Breakfast

A cheery breakfast room shares the main floor with the library. Light oak tables, a brick fireplace, and lace curtains create a welcoming atmosphere. Coffee is available starting at 7:30 a.m.; breakfast is served from 8 to 9:30 a.m.

The inn's cook, Ginnie, prepares a delightful meal from the open kitchen, and peers over the counter to chat with guests. Her farm on Cortes Island produces most of the fruit used in the inn's homemade jams. For starters, freshly baked muffins or coffeecake wait in baskets on the table. Next, guests feast on one of Ginnie's specials: eggs Florentine, baked eggs with smoked salmon and asparagus, or seasonal omelettes. Ginnie, who is used to cooking for a large family, believes in using only the freshest ingredients.

A picnic hamper may be ordered for lunch. A wicker basket lunch may include paté, cheese, fresh bread, cookies, fruit and wine or juice. Baskets should be ordered the night before.

In the Heart of Victoria

Abigail's location is ideal for exploring Victoria on foot. Just three blocks to the north, on Fort Street, there is a broad assortment of antique shops, for which Victoria is known. Auctions take place Tuesday and Friday evenings, and are likely to produce a real find for the collector.

Stroll along Government Street near the Inner Harbour for a look at many of Victoria's shops. Munro's Books, one of Canada's largest independent bookstores, displays its many volumes in a restored historic building. Straith's, also on Government Street, is noted for its fine tailored clothing. Irish linens, tartans and native British Columbian art are among the many other shopping treasures.

A short drive from Abigails, on Rockland Street, is the Lt. Governor's Mansion. The well-maintained grounds are open to the public. Visit the Art Gallery of Greater Victoria, 1040 Moss Street, featuring one of the finest Japanese art collections in Canada. Nearby is the Craigcarroch Castle, built in 1851 by Robert Dunsmuir for his wife. It features 36 rooms and leaded glass windows imported from Italy.

The Canterbury Bell bathroom combines antiques with a modern jacuzzi.

The Emily Carr Gallery, in the 106-year-old Rithet Building at 1107 Wharf Street, pays tribute to the world renowned Victoria artist. A film introduces the "Laughing One's" life and work. The artist's original work and manuscripts, her colorful impressions of the sea, mountains and village scenes of the West Coast Indians are displayed.

For a visit to a neighborhood pub, try Spinnakers located on Lime Bay at the foot of Catherine Street. The pub is known for its home brewed ales and stouts. Hearty pub fare completes the old English spirit. Abigail's staff can provide maps for attractions throughout the southern end of the island.

Getting There

From the Inner Harbour head north on Government Street. Take an immediate right onto Humboldt Street. Continue four blocks to Vancouver Street. Turn left onto Vancouver and continue four and one-half blocks to McClure. Turn left. Abigail's is at the end of the cul-de-sac.

BEACONSFIELD INN

Address:	998 Humboldt Street, Victoria, B.C. V8V 2Z8
Telephone:	(604) 384-4044
Location:	A few blocks from downtown Victoria
Host:	Hazel Prior, Innkeeper
Room Rates:	$90 to $175 (Canadian) $85 to $150 (U.S.) two persons
Credit Cards:	MasterCard, Visa
Remarks:	No pets. Rates include breakfast

The first thing you notice as you mount the steps to the stately Beaconsfield Inn is the sign which reads "City of Victoria Heritage Building." Next, as you pass through double doors etched with a grand peacock, you enter a black-and-white tiled sun room appointed with wicker furniture, stained glass, and huge potted plants. Passing through another set of doors, you are suddenly in an entryway of high ceilings, dark polished mahogany floors, antique stuffed birds and massive furniture. It is a step into another world — the Edwardian Period, "the height of the British Empire," during which clean, balanced lines created an elegant simplicity.

A Wedding Gift

Beaconsfield Inn was built by millionaire R.P. Rithet in 1905 as a wedding gift for his only daughter. The Edwardian mansion has been restored to its former elegance and carefully designed to portray the feeling of the era. Its decor reflects the tastes of the wealthy class who were reacting against the busy frivolity of the Victorian period.

Situated on a corner in a residential area near the heart of Victoria, Beaconsfield was at one time a nursing home. Purchased in 1973 by Bill McKechnie, it underwent serious renovation to return the building to its original design. The architectural drawings were retrieved from the University of Victoria's archives, and Bill scoured antique auctions for the ideal mix of furnishings in keeping with the design.

Edwardian Mansion

Each of the inn's 12 guest rooms is decorated to retain the design of a "typical" Edwardian mansion. A few of the rooms are named for individuals who were prominent during the period. For instance, there is an Oscar Wilde room and

Other names reflect the tone or feature of the room, such as the Rosebud Room, painted with pale rose and cream hues; the Blue Room, most definitely blue, with an alcove; or the Verandah Room, with its vintage wicker parlor furniture. All rooms have an elaborate private bath, down comforter and extended double or queen-size bed. The largest room, the Attic Suite, has a wet bar, private jacuzzi , fireplace and canopy bed. The Garden Suite, located on street level, opens onto an enclosed manicured garden, as does the smaller Gatekeeper Room. The smallest room is Willy's Room, which is cozy, but well suited to budget travel. Special touches add a personal note. Concierge service, fresh flowers, and an evening hot water bottle on request. For honeymooners, there may be a complimentary bottle of champagne.

The library is lined with leather furniture and extensive volumes of literature. Polished dark wood beams enhance the illusion that you have stepped into another era. An evening sherry hour in the library provides a chance to meet other guests. An inlaid wood table is the place for backgammon or chess.

Breakfast — coffee and juice, home baked goods and a daily entrée — is taken in the bright kitchen, served family style around an oak table. Eggs Beaconsfield, the cook's version of eggs Benedict, is a popular dish. Another favorite is salmon quiche.

As guests linger over fresh, hot coffee, they are apt to share travel tales and tips. Beaconsfield lends itself to this kind of relaxation and comraderie. Guests have a tendency to return to Beaconsfield again and again; the cards and letters displayed in the lobby give witness to their praise: "Absolutely fabulous. Great room, super breakfast. Marvelous."

Outside the Inn

Beaconsfield's location is ideal for seeing Victoria, and the innkeeper will gladly direct you. The British Columbia Provincial Museum is not far away. This world famous museum explores 12,000 years of natural and cultural history. A highlight features a recreation of a pioneer town, a coal mine shaft, a fish cannery, and Captain Cook's private cabin aboard his ship the *Discovery*. The newest exhibit features The Mysterious World of the Open Ocean. Explore the rich Indian cultural heritage of the Province's First Peoples in a stunning display of totem poles, masks and a Kwakuitl bighouse.

Victoria is a walking town, so simply taking a walk through one of the many parks is sure to liven your spirits. A lookout station at Beacon Hill Park, 184 acres of windswept knolls and colorful flower gardens, promises views of the ocean and mountains.

Golf is a year-round sport in Victoria at Glen Meadows Golf and Country Club on McTavish Road. At 6,800 yards, it is one of the longest courses in British Columbia. The Victoria Golf Club's spectacular 18-hole course overlooks the

The evening sherry hour takes place in the richly furnished library.

Strait of Juan de Fuca. The Cedar Hill Municipal Course features narrow fairways with several tees providing splendid views of downtown Victoria.

Drive along Beach Drive for another view of the Strait, and continue through Oak Bay to see the most handsome residential areas in the city. For a longer trip, drive north on Douglas Street through Goldstream Park to Malahat Drive. This route provides outstanding views of Mill Bay, Cowichan Bay, and the Gulf Islands in the distance.

Getting There

Follow Government Street along the Inner Harbor. Just past the Empress Hotel, turn right onto Humboldt Street. Cross Douglas, veering right. Continue for four blocks. The inn will be on a corner to your left.

CHEZ DANIEL

Address:	2522 Estevan Avenue, Victoria, B.C. V8R 2S7
Telephone:	(604) 592-7424
Host:	Daniel Rigollet, Owner, Chef de Cuisine
Cuisine:	Classic French with Nouvelle Cuisine
Prices:	Entrees $11 to $19.50 (Canadian)
Credit Cards:	MasterCard, Visa
Hours:	5:30 to 10 p.m. Tuesday through Saturday. Closed Sunday, Monday and Canadian holidays.

The inauspicious exterior of Chez Daniel may be somewhat misleading. Tucked in a small group of up-scale shops on a quiet street of northeast Victoria, the paned windows and lace curtains are only vague clues as to what awaits inside. Those who know, don't let on.

Chez Daniel is an intimate, very sophisticated, very French restaurant owned and operated by Daniel Rigollet. He also prepares its cuisine. Chef Daniel is a member of the world's oldest guild for masters of cuisine, the Confrerie de la Chaine des Rotisseurs; his meals are the culmination of his culinary experience in France, Switzerland, Germany, Ireland, and the Netherlands.

Daniel combs the Victoria markets early each morning to obtain his high-quality ingredients. His prevailing attitude: continually strive toward perfection. The charming, gracious chef uses only the freshest foods, and the quality is evident in his dishes.

Two candlelit dining rooms, each decorated in a muted pallette of mauve and teal, accommodate an intimate number of diners. Baroque music and rich kitchen aromas create a pleasing atmosphere. Guests are greeted warmly; the waitstaff upholds the finest standards of service, delivering a cheery "Bon appétit" with the commencement of your meal.

Very Fresh, Very French

Begin with one of Chez Daniel's appetizers such as fresh sauteed mushrooms, escargots with garlic butter, sweetbreads with mushrooms and port in a puff pastry. Daniel's "soup a l'oignon, au gratin" is a fresh rendition of the traditional soup. Salad with hearts of palm and artichoke is the perfect intermezzo before the main course. "Salade Ceasar" is artfully prepared at your table.

Daniel's broad selection of entrées may make it difficult to choose just one. Salmon with Noilly Prat and cream and fresh trout with almonds lead the fish section. Fresh prawns, sautéed in butter and topped with tomato and a dash of garlic is another popular selection. A special "Rable de Lapereau 'Hussarde'" (loin of rabbit) is prepared for parties of two, and young rabbit in a white wine sauce is a delectable alternative. Fresh lamb with a ginger, shallot, brandy, cream sauce is one of Daniel's favorites.

Chez Daniel's wine list includes some 290 selections from Australia, California, Canada, France and Germany. Fine champagnes round out the cellar.

Homemade fresh fruit sorbets are an excellent, light finale. A tray of cheese, mostly imported, is offered in keeping with the French tradition. The dessert tray is hard to resist, though, with its chocolate truffles, creme caramel Chantilly, and Floating Islands.

Teas, including herbal blends, and espresso cap off the evening. Chez Daniel also serves a variety of dessert "special" coffees, including the Chez Daniel café, with five liqueurs, and a choice of select ports, cognacs and digestives.

Getting There

Take Fort Street East until it becomes Cadboro Bay Road. Continue to Estevan Avenue and turn right. For a more leisurely drive, travel along Dallas Road and Beach Drive past Sealand and turn left on Estevan.

Daniel Rigollet is both chef and host.

SOOKE HARBOUR HOUSE

Address:	1528 Whiffen Spit Road, Rural Route 4, Sooke, B.C. V0S 1N0
Telephone:	(604) 642-3421 or 642-4944
Location:	Twenty-three miles west of Victoria
Hosts:	Fredrica and Sinclair Philip
Room Rates:	Approximately $77 to $200 (U.S.)
Credit Cards:	American Express, MasterCard, Visa
Remarks:	Breakfast and light lunch included in room rate. Reservations recommended. Lunch served to hotel guests only.

If ever an inn was created to lull life's tempo back to a natural adagio, it's Sooke Harbour House. This trim, white elegant inn rests just above Sooke Harbour's Whiffen Spit. Broad views of the Straits of Juan de Fuca and Washington's Olympic Mountains are seen through the inn's picture windows. Below, an ever-changing landscape of tidal pools, kelp beds, and natural driftwood sculptures create a living mural.

Stitching the many fabrics of Sooke Harbour House together are Fredrica and Sinclair Philip. Fredrica, born in Cannes, France, radiates a refined warmth. Dressed in her crisp French frocks, she graciously manages the workings of the inn as well as the raising of their four children. Sinclair, a native of Vancouver, holds a doctorate in political economics from the University of Grenoble, where he and Fredrica met. He is well-studied in wines and foods, and an expert Northwest seafood chef.

World Class Dining

Colorful gardens ring the inn. Although it may seem odd to see Sinclair snatch a crimson petal from a poppy and take a bite out of it, guests themselves are soon enough nibbling on pansies, pineapple sage, Corsican mint, or any of the gifts from the inn's 400 varieties of herbs, flowers, berries and fruit trees — over 95% of the gardens on their grounds are edible, and most of it ends up on the menu. The ocean realm, too, offers prodigious harvests of delicacies such as octopus, sea urchin, gooseneck barnacle, periwinkles and whelks. Under the spell of Sooke's masterful chefs, the land and sea gardens blend to create the freshest and most innovative cuisine in British Columbia. Ann Hardy's renowned national guidebook *Where to Eat in Canada*, has just awarded the inn's restaurant three stars as one of Canada's top eight restaurants for the third consecutive year and Country Inn's Magazine named it one of North America's top ten inns.

Skin Dives Daily.

Here, when they say seasonally, they mean daily. Sinclair, an avid scuba diver, harvests the rich bounties of their watery front yard for the evening's meal. The inn's commercial fishing boat supplies fish and crab to create a menu that changes daily. Sinclair, Fredrica, Pia Carroll, and Ron Cherry share the chef's duties. Each is an artist with food as their medium.

Fresh sea urchin roe and fresh sea cucumber may appear as appetizers. Fresh steamed sablefish with an anise-hyssop butter sauce, or fresh skate sautéed with a cranberry vinegar sauce may be among the choice of entrées. More traditional seafood dishes are always available, as well as local, organically grown meats such as rabbit, veal, lamb, duck, guinea hen and venison.

Ideal for Honeymoon and Romance

Sooke Harbour House, like its cuisine, is an exquisite mingling of traditional North American country sensibilities and West Coast native design. The New House, completed in 1986, offers ten distinctly different, definitely divine rooms. Each is named and decorated with a theme. All have an expansive ocean view and private balcony or terrace. In each room, a comfortable sitting area faces a fireplace which is made and ready to be used.

One of the most coveted rooms of the assemblage is the Victor Newman Longhouse, named for the Sooke carver of its many Indian masks and rare hand carved Chieftain's bench. This large room features a king-size bed and bath tub for two. The whirlpool is situated next to a see-through fireplace, that lends a view of Sooke Bay and the mountains beyond. Outdoor whirlpools are found on the decks of the Mermaid Room and the Underwater Orchard. Both have stunning views through their own private gardens by the ocean. The Icthyologist's study, sometimes referred to as the "Fish Room," is a veritable aquarium of fish art, including hand painted fish tiles, fish prints, fish rubbings, and fish weavings. As in many of the other rooms, hand painted tiles are also found in the Edible Blossom Room, where taking a shower is really a botany lesson in disguise.

The Sooke Harbour House bears all the charm of an airy French auberge. The three bedrooms in the old house are furnished with antiques, handmade flower wreaths and handsewn quilts. The split-level Blue Heron features a king-size bed, spacious sun deck, and perhaps the best view from the Inn, while in the whirlpool tub for two, warmed by the nearby fireplace.

Whiffen Spit, Beaches and Trails

To explore the Sooke Harbour House's world of wonders, begin with a walk along Whiffen Spit. Bald eagles nest nearby, while herons, sandpipers, loons and cormorants frequent the area. Killer whales, seals and sea lions feed just

Fredrica and Sinclair Philip serve only the freshest available foods.

offshore as well as the "resident" year-round grey whale. The inn's staff will arrange for scuba diving, kayaking, or windsurfer and fishing charter rentals. Nature walks can be arranged with ethnobotonists, or local guide and bilingual staff member, Michel Jensen-Reynaud. The area is ideal for photography; horses nearby are also available for rent.

The West Coast Life Saving Trail and Pacific Rim National Park begin at the road's end near Port Renfrew and extend nearly 100 miles along the coast, offering excellent hiking opportunities. The trail originally was constructed as a means of rescuing shipwrecked mariners. Surfers ride the waves at nearby Jordan River.

Getting There

From Victoria, follow Highway 1 North to the Highway 14 intersection. Follow signs to Sooke. Approximately one mile from the stoplight in Sooke, turn left onto Whiffen Spit Road. Follow it to the water, where the Sooke Harbour House is on your right at the ocean's edge.

HASTINGS HOUSE

Address: P.O. Box 1110, Ganges, B.C., Canada V0S 1E0
Telephone: (604) 537-2362, reservations (800) 661-9255, from Western Canada and the United States
Location: Salt Spring Island, Canadian Gulf Islands
Hosts: Pamela and Hector de Galard.
Rates: $230 to $360 double, $180 to $290 off-season (Canadian). Each additional person $25. Breakfast and afternoon tea included. Rates are subject to change.
Credit Cards: American Express, Mastercard, VISA.
Remarks: Minimum stay of two nights on weekends in July and August; three nights on holiday weekends. Closed December, January 2 – February 13.

Hastings House is located on 30 acres of Salt Spring Island's forested, lush meadow land. An adult retreat of the highest calibre, it bears a striking resemblance to an English farm estate. Designed and built in 1942 by Warren Hastings, a naval architect, the Manor House is, in fact, a replica of his family home in Sussex.

Country Estate

Six handsome buildings comprise the country estate—the largest, the white half-timbered Manor House, being the focal point, leaded glass windows, beamed ceilings, wooden floors, and antiques, along with soft classical music, create an elegant atmosphere. Upstairs, a library nook and two seaview suites await, each with two bedrooms and full bath. Fragrant English roses climb outside the windows of one suite. In the living room a huge inglenook contains a cowled, brick fireplace. Here, afternoon tea is served. Sharing the main floor is the dining room.

The most deluxe suites are in the Farm House, overlooking the harbour. Each contains a king size bed upstairs and a sitting room with an open brick fireplace downstairs. Two full bathrooms and front and back porches are found in each suite.

Post Cottage, the first Hudson Bay Post on Salt Spring Island, is situated under a pear tree in the nearby orchard. Wicker furniture, a wood stove, and floral batiks accent the cozy cabin. French doors open to the manicured

lawns. Just beyond the Cottage, the Barn features two parlor suites and two bed sitting rooms.

Cliffsdale and Ivy are located on an adjacent bluff, overlooking the harbour. The two bedroom suite at Cliffsdale features a large living room and an outside deck. Ivy, downstairs from Cliffsdale, is a bright and attractive one-room suite.

Most suites have a wet bar, refridgerator, fireplace, and private telephone. Down quilts, fresh flowers, plants, oversized towels, fine imported soaps, and terry robes enhance the atmosphere of luxury.

Hastings House is a noted conference retreat. The Mews conference facility will accomodate up to 14 people, and is outfitted with audio-visual equipment.

Special Touches

The moment guests arrive, the pampering begins. The staff attends to all the little touches. A nameplate appears on the door of your room. A thermos of hot coffee arrives with baked goods in a quilted hamper each morning. Your dinner menu is personalized in calligraphy. And, while you dine, your room is straightened, the fire laid, and fresh towels are put out.

Dining in the quiet elegance of the Manor House is as much a treat as are the accomodations. The Chef creates imaginative cuisine, with a French influence that produces true dining adventure. Menus change daily and the use of local fresh produce and seafood is stressed. Fresh eggs are collected from the hen house daily and the Chef can be seen selecting produce from the garden. Vegetables and fruit are grown on the estate; jams and jellies are homemade, including the specialties of blackberry and apricot.

Dinner is served at 7:00 p.m. and must be reserved prior to 1:00 p.m. of the same day. From the dining room, guests retire to the living room for coffee and liqueurs by the stone fireplace. (Warren Hastings buried an earthenware pot under the hearth to ward off witches, according to Sussex custom.)

Breakfast is served in the dining room to guests only. A la carte luncheons and Sunday brunch are open to the public. Reservations are suggested.

Tranquil Island

Salt Spring boasts a "cool Mediterranean" climate due to favorable Japanese currents, so year round activities are available. Locals call this area the "Hawaii" of Canada. Tranquil atmosphere prevails at Hastings House and on Salt Spring Island, and guests are encouraged to relax in the peaceful solitude. Hastings House itself offers the use of bicycles and croquet equipment. Boat rentals, fishing, sailing, golfing, and tennis are all within easy walking distance of Hastings House.

The huge inglenook contains a cowled brick fireplace..

The town of Ganges, a five minute walk from the estate, is lined with excellent galleries and shops. Local artisans are known for oil and watercolor paintings, pottery, carvings, weavings, and stained glass. A farmer's market each Saturday, a salmon derby, jazz festival, performing arts theatre, and golf tournament are further ways to enjoy the island. Hiking and beachcombing are always popular pursuits. picnic lunches may be requested from the dining room for all-day excursions.

If you arrive by private boat, you can moor at the marina.

Getting There

Salt Spring Island is serviced daily by B.C. Ferries from Tsawwassen, Swartz Bay and Crofton, and by float plane from Vancouver. Arrangements can be made to meet guests at the ferry terminals and the float plane dock

THE OLD HOUSE RESTAURANT

Address: 1760 Riverside Lane, Courtenay, B.C. V9N 8C7
Telephone: (604) 338-5406
Host: Michael McLaughlin, Owner
Cuisine: Continental
Prices: Entrees $10.95 to $17.95 upstairs and $4.95 to $13.95 downstairs (Canadian)
Hours: 11:30 a.m. to 9 p.m. daily, upstairs opens at 5:30 p.m. and is closed Sunday and Monday (Monday in summer only). Sunday brunch served 10:00 a.m. to 2 p.m.
Remarks: Reservations upstairs strongly recommended.

The town of Courtenay, in the vast Comox Valley, is situated mid-way along Vancouver Island's eastern flank. The Courtenay River meanders through the valley, its mild waters passing farms, mills and homes. In 1938, along the river's then wild banks, the pioneering Kirk Family built their home on four acres of the loveliest land in the valley. In 1973, it was purchased by Michael McLaughlin and transformed, over a matter of six months, into a premier dining spot — The Old House Restaurant.

"At the Old House," says Mike, "we aim to create an all-around enjoyable experience, which includes the grounds, buildings and people. Food is the primary reason people come here, but the surroundings certainly enhance the whole feeling."

The Old House is essentially two restaurants sharing one roof. Entering on the ground floor, one is reminded of a lively English pub. A stone fireplace and heavy beams lend a lodge atmosphere which is popular with aprés-ski and aprés-anything crowds. Meals are moderately priced, and feature robust pub-style sandwiches, salads, pastas, and local seafood specialties.

Upstairs at the Old House one finds a more elegant dining room, lit with coal-oil lanterns and warmed by a fire. Open timbers are accented by skylights and hanging plants. Leaded windows offer views of the river and the grounds

Specialties of the House

The chefs glean the finest of local ingredients from Comox Valley farmers and fishermen to create their array of dishes. Begin the meal with a soup such as Cream of Pheasant and Black Beans (with wild mushrooms, cranberry cream, and a touch of gin). Salads are innovative as well—the Butter Lettuce and Scallop Seviche salad is embellished with oyster mushrooms, scallions, pinenuts, and a raspberry vinagrette. The Old House's entrees may include Medallions of Venison, Prawns with Black Spatzle, or a specially prepared

Partridge dish. An extensive wine list features European, Canadian, and American vintages. The smokehouse is in constant use preparing the smoked meats and fish that are complimented by the fresh herbs grown in the garden.

The Old House offers lunch selections such as gourmet salads, soups, sandwiches and intriguing items like Seafarer's Schnitzel and ploughman's traditional pub fare. The country style brunch is a feast ranging from Honey Glazed Camenbert with Almonds to Seafood St. Jacques. Each day, time is set aside for afternoon tea.

On the Grounds

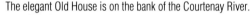

The beautifully manicured grounds are ideal for a stroll following a meal. A small gazebo, on the river's bank, offers a place to watch seals, otters and blue herons. Weddings are also held here. Just behind the restaurant is Dower Cottage, offering jewelry, gifts, home decorations, and collectibles.

Getting There

From Nanaimo, drive north on Highway 19. Entering Courtenay, turn right on 17th Street. Before crossing the bridge, turn right again on Riverside. The Old House is just ahead on your left.

The elegant Old House is on the bank of the Courtenay River.

APRIL POINT LODGE

Address: Box 1, Campbell River, B.C. V9W 4Z9
Telephone: (604) 285-2222
Location: On Quadra Island, off Campbell River on the northeastern coast of Vancouver Island
Hosts: Phyllis, Warren, Eric, Carl, Mark, Joy, Heidi and Troy Peterson
Room Rates: $119 to $189 (Canadian), $25 each additional person. Guests under 16 stay free. Two- and three-bedroom suites from $350; three- to five-bedroom guest houses from $395.
Credit Cards: American Express, MasterCard, Visa
Remarks: All meals — à la carte except packages. Open April through October.

The phrase "Nice fish" echoes across Discovery Passage, bounces off Vancouver Island, and lands firmly on the dock at April Point Lodge where veteran anglers knowingly refer to the Lodge as the home of "legendary fishing."

April Point Lodge is a world-class resort that stretches along three and one-half miles of shoreline on Quadra Island. Over 200 acres of coastal forest lands surround the main lodge and its guest cabins. Constructed by the Peterson family in 1944, the lodge is still run by brothers Eric and Warren, and their lively 80-year-old mother, Phyllis. Today's refined lodge emerged from ramshackle dwellings on what had been called Poverty Point.

The handsome main lodge is the communal gathering place. It houses the dining room, lounge, office, and a handful of guest rooms. Suites within the lodge feature a living room, fireplace and sun deck. Spacious studios in the main lodge and guest lodges, as well as two- to five-bedroom cabins, are available. April Point's lodgings all offer a view of the water and private bath. Some include a fireplace, kitchenette and hot tub.

Total Fishing

From May through October, the nurturing waters around April Point are obliging host to meaty salmon, cod and perch. Early season yields bluebacks, or immature Coho, which continue to grow until mid-September when they may weigh up to 22 pounds. Chinook are in large throngs by late May, and escalate to as much as 40 to 60 pounds by mid-summer. Fishing carries well into October.

April Point maintains the largest privately owned fleet of Boston Whalers (about 55) in the world. Ranging from 13 to 21 feet in length, these swift craft carry guests from the lodge's docks into the abundant waters of Discovery Passage, the Campbell River, and Seymour Narrows. The staff of 50 highly experienced guides are what make the fishing fun and fruitful. With strong hands-on experience, and a thorough development program at the lodge, these guides rank among the most respected in British Columbia, if not the world. In addition to vast knowledge of fishing techniques, they are well versed in local history, Indian fishing methods and food preparation, safety, and marine life management.

Generally, guides fish with the guests for the duration of the week. Guided trips cost $45 to $55 per hour for two people, with a four hour minimum. Cost includes the boat, guide, tackle and fuel. It is customary to tip the guide, either daily or at the end of the week. The week's catch may be frozen and packaged for travel, or a local firm will can or smoke it for you.

Fresh Air Appetites

A day of fishing, or just breathing the fresh salt water air, builds a healthy appetite. Fortunately, April Point prides itself on quality dining. The fresh seafood selections are naturally extensive, and change daily depending on local catches. Dungeness crab, served cracked with drawn butter, is a standard item. Prawns, ling cod and snapper are frequent bestsellers, as is, of course, salmon. Should you choose, the kitchen will prepare your very own salmon, in a festive fashion, and serve it to you in the dining room for a minimal fee. Rack of lamb and prime rib, as well as outdoor steak barbeques round out the entrées. Lunches are primarily soups and sandwiches, while breakfast is simply not breakfast without one of "Mrs. P's" stickie buns.

The dining room, with its Northwest Coast Indian masks and cedar beams, overlooks Discovery Passage. At night, freighters and cruise ships pass by, while in the daylight seals, whales and eagles may be seen. Guests gather in the cozy bar before dinner to swap fishing tales, and around the fire afterwards to set the records straight.

Beside the Point

Quadra Island boasts a strong Indian heritage which bears exploration. One of the oldest original Kwakiutl Indian villages lies near the lodge and has a fascinating historical museum. At Cape Mudge an ancient petroglyph site is well worth the visit. Rebecca Spit, on the east side of the island, offers stunning mountain views. Beachcombing, clam digging, oyster picking, swimming and hiking are accessible from the lodge. Boating picnics may also be arranged. The kitchen will prepare a gourmet picnic hamper for you and your guide to enjoy on a beach, complete with linens, silver, and fine wine. Cracked crab or Cornish hens are two of the movable feasts.

Spacious suites come with waterside decks.

The Petersons can arrange a guided hike to discover many of the Indian Petroglyph sites, some of which are only found at low tide. For a real surprise ask about "swimming with the salmon" in the Campbell River.

Getting There

To reach April Point by car, drive one hundred and sixty miles north of Victoria to Campbell River. Take the Quadra Island ferry, which runs nearly every half-hour. Follow Pidcock Road to the lodge. To fly, scheduled air service is available from Vancouver to Campbell River, then take water taxi or limosine service to the lodge. From Sea-Tac airport in Seattle, you can make arrangements with Float Plane Services to pick you up at the airport and drive you to downtown Seattle where their float planes are moored. From there it's a two-hour flight directly to the lodge.

PARK ROYAL HOTEL

Address:	540 Clyde Avenue, West Vancouver, B.C. V7T 2J7
Telephone:	(604) 926-5511
Lication:	In West Vancouver, just north of the Lion's Gate Bridge
Host:	Mario Corsi, Manager
Room Rates:	$74 to $185 (Canadian)
Credit Cards:	American Express, Carte Blanche, Diners Club, MasterCard, Visa
Remarks:	Coffee or tea and morning newspaper delivered to room, complimentary.

"The Park Royal is a country style inn found in a busy metropolis," says host Mario Corsi. "It's cozy, and has a staff who really care about the comfort of the guests." Mario should know; after all, most of his staff have been with him for a good part of his 15 years as manager of the hotel. Mario's European upbringing and hotel training have led him to create a high standard of service and quality reminiscent of a Continental hotel. "Nothing phony or glitzy," he says proudly. "Just a good feeling, like being in a little village. The problem with lots of hotels these days is that there is no surprise." That philosophy and Mario's enthusiasm are what make the Park Royal such a rare find in a city of more than 1.2 million. This hotel is delightfully different.

On the River Bank

Located on the north side of Vancouver's harbor, just minutes from the bustling downtown area, the Tudor style, ivy festooned hotel provides a quiet retreat for the business or vacation traveler. The two-story building is surrounded by trimmed lawns and flower beds. The Capilano River runs just outside. Twelve of the inn's 30 rooms face the river and overlook the gardens. On quiet nights you can open the window and be lulled to sleep by the rushing water. Most rooms offer queen or double beds; a few have twins. All rooms have private baths, and are individually decorated with floral print wallpapers, antique oak furniture, and leaded glass windows. A large suite offers a jacuzzi, VCR, plush terry robes and a wet bar. (Future plans call for the addition of more rooms of this caliber.) The morning newspaper and coffee or tea are delivered to your room upon request. These are just a few of the touches that lend Park Royal its intimacy.

A Lively Pub

An authentic English pub downstairs offers lively piano entertainment Monday through Saturday evenings. The piano player has been playing at the pub

for years despite his youth, and is rarely ever stumped when you call out a request. Pubsters may just be tempted to belt out a favorite melody in this intimate lounge.

Public rooms are paneled in dark woods. Flowered and scenic print draperies hang on the windows. A big stone fireplace, set with a crackling fire, is especially cheery on a damp Vancouver evening in winter.

Dining In Style

Park Royal is as proud of its restaurant as it is of its rooms. The Tudor Room is regarded as one of the top dining spots in the city. Regional specialties and old standards combine to create a diverse menu with wide appeal. Hans Schaub, chef here for 12 years, prides himself on freshness and consistency of product. The dining room overlooks the garden, and is warmly appointed with tapestry-covered chairs, vintage prints and stained glass. Dinner entrées include breast of pheasant with red currants and brandy, black pasta with smoked salmon, red caviar and cream, and traditional favorites such as beef Wellington and Châteaubriand. A resident baker supplies fresh breads and stunning desserts.

Breakfast and lunch selections are as noteworthy as dinner. Begin the day with huevos rancheros or eggs Park Royal (poached eggs, smoked salmon, salmon caviar and Hollandaise sauce). Lunch offers a steak and kidney pie, scallops in a fresh basil cream, or veal scaloppine.

Herbs from the inn's year-round greenhouse are used in the cuisine, giving a bright, fresh taste. In warm weather, lunch, cocktails and snacks may be taken on the secluded patio off the dining room.

Exploring the "Other" Vancouvers

Park Royal is located in West Vancouver, just a few minutes walk from the Park Royal Shopping Center. Over 190 shops are found in this trendy mall, including three of Canada's top department stores: The Bay, Eaton's and Woodward's. Ambleside Park stretches along the shore behind the mall, and may be reached by following a trail outside the Park Royal Hotel.

North Vancouver offers additional opportunities for exploration. Grouse Mountain is a favorite destination in any season. Two aerial tramways depart for the mountaintop every 15 minutes, 10 a.m. to 10 p.m., offering spectacular views of the city and environs. Mountain meadows, paved walking paths, and the Blue Grouse Lake and nature trails offer excellent hiking for all fitness levels. In winter, four double chair lifts and two T-bars carry skiers to the 4,100-foot peak. Helicopter tours are available for reaching even greater heights. To get there, take Marine Drive to Capilano Road. Head north on Capilano to Grouse Mountain.

The elegant Tudor Room overlooks the gardens and the Capilano River.

En route to the mountain, visit the Capilano Suspension Bridge and Park. Constructed of wire rope with wood decking, the bridge stretches four hundred and fifty feet across the canyon, some two hundred and thirty feet above the river. At night, illumination adds to the spectacle. Crossing the bridge you may view Coho and Chinook salmon on their upriver swim to the Capilano Hatchery. The west side park contains trout and salmon ponds, historical and botanical trails.

North Vancouver's newest waterfront attraction is Lonsdale Quay Market. A bustling public market with boutiques and shops, restaurants and cafes, the area also offers a prime view of Vancouver and the harbor.

Getting There

Follow Georgia Street through Vancouver across the Lion's Gate Bridge. Take West Vancouver Exit, turn left on Marine Drive and right on Taylor Way, then right onto Clyde Avenue. Go one block. Turn right, the hotel is on the left. Free parking is available. From Trans-Canada 1 turn off at Exit 1 (Taylor Way-Vancouver), go downhill to Clyde Avenue and turn left at the Park Royal sign.

CORSI TRATTORIA

Address:	1 Lonsdale, Vancouver, B.C. V7M 2E4
Telephone:	(604) 987-9910
Hosts:	Mario and Antonio Corsi, Owners
Cuisine:	Italian
Prices:	Entrees $6.95 to $13.95 (Canadian)
Credit Cards:	American Express, Diners Club, MasterCard, Visa
Remarks:	Reservations recommended.

Corsi Trattoria, located on North Vancouver's waterfront across from the new Lonsdale Quay Market development and the SeaBus to downtown Vancouver, offers Italian cuisine in an authentic Mediterranean atmosphere. A bright green awning outside yields to the white stucco and terra cotta inside. Burgundy and pink linens, candles and photographs lend a cozy feeling. "You can go in blue jeans or a long gown," says co-owner Mario Corsi.

The Corsi brothers, Mario and Antonio, have been in the restaurant and hotel business since their childhood, when their family ran a small hotel outside Rome. "It's not just our business," Mario says,"it's our life."

Both brothers are involved in the restaurant, and Antonio is chef. "He is always in and out of the kitchen talking to guests," says Mario. "It's simple, the way a trattoria should be," says Antonio. "We put our effort into the food, service and atmosphere and work at making everyone feel at home."

A Classic

Corsi Trattoria blends the finest of central Italian cuisine with the freshest of West Coast ingredients. Ever conscious of fine ingredients, the restaurant orders its veal from a special source in Montreal. Fish and fowl are carefully selected from local markets.

Classic dishes include a wide variety of antipasto, as well as over 50 pasta specialties. Fettuccine, gnocchetti, spaghetti, fusilli, bucatini and capelli d'angelo are among the pastas made fresh daily on the premises. Featured entrées are penne all'Arrabiata (spicy tomato sauce with bacon and Romano cheese), and spinach fettucine with cream, ham and mushrooms.

For lunch, you might have antipasto of mozzarella in carrozza (fried mozzarella in tomato sauce), rotollo a las Corsi (pasta stuffed with spinach, ham and cheese), pasta salad with shrimp or steamed clams.

Beyond Pasta

Though Corsi Trattoria is noted for its pasta dishes, the menu extends far beyond. Non-pasta dishes include prawns, pan fried in butter and sprinkled with oregano and white vermouth, or a veal scallopine in an apple and cream sauce. Fritto misto (lightly breaded fried prawns, mussels and squid) is also a popular dish. Accompanying vegetables arrive perfectly *al dente* on side plates. Dinner salads include spinach and mushroom, mixed greens or fresh mozzarella and tomato.

For dessert: creme caramel, zabaglione and zuccotto, an Italian chocolate cake are a few of the options. An almost entirely Italian wine list offers selections in many price ranges.

The most popular item on the menu is a feast of five different pastas in an array of sauces (minimum of two orders). "L'Abbuffata" includes four different pastas, a mixed salad, lamb, veal piccata, prawns, zabaglione and espresso (also a minimum of two orders).

Getting There

Go east on Marine Drive to Lonsdale. Turn right. The restaurant is located on the last right corner. There is plenty of parking nearby.

Some of the pasta is "for Italians only.".

BISHOPS

Address:	2183 W. Fourth Avenue, Vancouver, B.C.
Telephone:	(604) 738-2025
Location:	Kitsilano
Hosts:	John and Linda Bishop
Prices:	Lunch entrees $9.95 to $12.95. Dinner entrees $9.95 to $21.95. (Canadian)
Credit Cards:	American Express, Diners Club, MasterCard, Visa
Hours:	Lunch is served Monday through Friday 11:30 am to 2:30 pm. Dinner is served Monday through Saturday 5:30 pm to 11 pm; Sunday 5:30 to 10 pm.

Owner John Bishop, a soft-spoken Welshman, designed his restaurant with subtle elegance. A bold pink neon sign, against an understated gray exterior, matter-of-factly announces Bishop's. Inside, the restaurant is dressed in the same simplicity. The pale gray walls are adorned by the works of local artists. "It's a clean, contemporary West Coast restaurant." says John. "Our emphasis is on elegant food, simply prepared with the freshest ingredients."

With a seasonal menu reflecting the best local products, Bishop's cuisine is in a class of its own. "It's not Californian or French or nouvelle anything." says John. "It's contemporary home cooking." Bishop's food is uniquely Bishop's.

Since opening four years ago, Bishop's has earned a respected place among Vancouver's leading restaurants.

Dessert First

It wouldn't be unusual to be tempted by the dessert menu even before the entree selections are considered. The restaurant's signature dessert—Death by Chocolate—is a decadent, dark chocolate paté, smothered with a brilliant raspberry sauce. It's an exceptional edible worth tasting.

To fully appreciate Bishop's, a more traditional approach to the menu is the way to go. Innovative appetizers can include smoked salmon on buckwheat noodles with vodka creme fraiche, or grilled bocconcini wrapped in proscuitto and romaine. Fresh shellfish, including steamed clams and grilled oysters with tamarind sauce, often accent the dinner menu. Daily soup selections range from wild mushroom broth to a substantial crab and corn chowder.

A quartet of pastas that might include delicate penne served with grilled eggplant, roasted peppers and basil pesto, or black pepper fettuccine cloaked in an exotic woodland mushroom sauce also enhance the evening menu.

Bishop's entrees feature a selection of fresh fish, veal, lamb and poultry simply prepared and served with fresh vegetables. Grilled local salmon is often punctuated with crushed black peppercorns. Roasted pork tenderloin may be embellished with a honey mustard sauce, while sauteed prawn tails marinate in tequila and lime. Fresh herbs and edible flowers are used in the artful presentation of each dish. Bread, baked daily on the premises, accompanies the meal.

Bishop's wine cellar is thoughtfully stocked with selections for most tastes and pocketbooks. John has even developed his own label featuring one of the paintings hanging in the restaurant. Future plans include more private labels. Bishop's features a full-service bar and a rich selection of dessert wines. Espresso drinks, regular and decaffeinated, are also available.

Service is always attentive at Bishop's. John and Linda can frequently be found circulating among the tables visiting with their guests. Soft jazz or classical music, candlelight and intimate tables make Bishop's a perfect place to enjoy a special meal in comfortable ambience.

Getting There

Traveling northbound on Oak Street, turn left on Broadway. Turn right on Yew. Bishop's is on the corner of Fourth and Yew.

Dine with John Bishop in his highly regarded restaurant.

THE WILLIAM TELL

Address: 765 Beattie Street, Vancouver, B.C. V6B 2M4
Telephone: (604) 688-3504
Host: Erwin Doebeli
Cuisine: Swiss Continental
Prices: Lunch entrees $7.75 to $10.75, dinner $18 to $23. (Canadian)
Credit Cards: American Express, Diners Club, MasterCard, Visa
Hours: Lunch 11:30 a.m. to 2 p.m. Monday-Friday; Dinner 6-10 p.m. daily.

The legendary hero William Tell is traditionally known for his strength and skill as a marksman — particularly when it came to shooting an arrow through the apple on his son's head. He represents the spirit of the movement toward Switzerland's independence, and is esteemed for his strength of character. In his honor, Swiss born Erwin Doebeli created Vancouver's William Tell Restaurant with the same high standards and spirit of independence.

Doebeli began his restaurant career in Switzerland, holding positions in every aspect of the trade. Emigrating to Canada in 1962 he continued to develop his knowledge and experience and opened the William Tell Restaurant in 1964. Over the years the menus changed, the locale improved, and the kitchen was modernized. In its near quarter-century of operation, the William Tell has achieved and maintained ratings as one of the finest restaurants in Canada.

The restaurant's impeccably dressed and well-trained staff deliver excellent service, while Doebeli himself circulates the dining room to greet guests and ensure their satisfaction.

The original restaurant was located on Richards Street. Five years ago it was moved to its much larger, more elegant quarters in the Georgian Court Hotel. The three cream-colored rooms have comfortably spaced tables covered with Swiss linens, oversized silver service, plates, and delicate fresh flower arrangements. Embossed napkins, silver flatware, and the large menus all bear the William Tell insignia, a crossbow motif.

Swiss Precision

William Tell's food and service are as carefully detailed as the decor. Chef Lars Trolle insists on the finest ingredients, and delivers a premium product. Five- and three-course *prix fixe* menus are offered in addition to the à la carte selections. These reflect seasonal variations and showcase new items. The restaurant's cuisine had, several years ago, been classified as conservative.

The new kitchen perhaps brought about a new outlook— its renderings are lighter and more imaginative than its predecessor.

The à la carte selections appeal to all tastes and appetites. Upon seating, complimentary puff pastries filled with salmon mousse are served. Hors d'oeuvres range from air-dried, Swiss style beef to leek and smoked goose breast in puff pastry. Salads are fresh and innovative, a favorite being "La Salade du Marché" (or today's choice from the market), which could be smoked pheasant or perhaps goose paté on curly endive.

A selection of fish, fowl and meats comprise the two-page entrée listings, including a filet of salmon in sorrel sauce, medallions of monkfish and prawns in saffron, and marinated rack of lamb with garlic and fresh herbs.

The lunch menu stresses soups, salads, and a choice of entrées ranging from Pacific salmon with pink peppercorn sauce to broiled filet mignon in a lively mustard sauce.

Getting There

From Vancouver's Georgia Street, heading east, turn right onto Cambie Street. Turn left on Robson, then left onto Beatty. The William Tell is in the Georgian Court Hotel directly across from B.C. Place.

Erwin Doebeli will be your host.

HATHEUME LAKE RESORT

Address:	P.O. Box 490, Peachland, B.C. V0H 1X0
Telephone:	June through September (604) 762-1148.
	(604) 767-2642 off season.
Location:	About one and one-half hours by unpaved road west
	of Peachland or east of Quilchena
Hosts:	Tim and Janet Tullis, Gus and Leni Averill
Room Rates:	$175 per day, $1,125 per week (Canadian) American
	Plan. Children from five to 12 are charge at
	two-thirds rate.
Credit Cards:	None
Remarks:	Reservations necessary.

Over the years, as trails and roads sliced farther into the interior of British Columbia, fishermen discovered a remote pocket of lakes known to native Indians as Hatheume, or "Big Fish." Of all fresh water game fish, none holds quite the reputation for size and fighting spirit as the Kamloops trout, a hardy strain of rainbow found almost exclusively in the isolated lakes that dot the forested Nicola Plateau, a high plateau wilderness situated between the Coastal Range and the Canadian Rockies. There's something about these thick woods and cold lakes that mends the soul. For those seeking peace and quiet in a remote setting, Hatheume Lake Resort is an excellent choice.

A Wilderness Retreat

Among the straight pine and quaking aspen along the shore of Lake Hatheume, you will find a splendid lodge and six comfortable cabins, all built of hand-hewn logs. For a few days, a week perhaps, guests can become part of the penetrating freshness of this rare wilderness. Each of the eight lakes that together make up the Hatheume Lake Resort still support resident loons and occasional deer, bear and moose can be seen as well.

The exuberant greeting from Gus Averill or his wife Leni is as genuine as the trout jumping out there in the lake. Then again, it may be Tim Tullis who comes from the dock to welcome you, or his wife Janet. That bottle of Okanagan wine in your cabin is just one of the ways they have of saying they're glad you've made it. Until the moment you leave, they and their very competent staff will do everything they can to make sure you're comfortable and content. The Averills and Tullises have plenty to do just keeping the equipment running and the meals coming, but they always seem to find time to give a fly casting lesson, brew a fresh pot of coffee or suggest spots for photography.

Clean and Homey

The facilities are basic, clean and homey. Each of the well-heated cabins has two large bedrooms with twin beds, a private bath with shower and a nicely furnished sitting room which looks out onto the lake. The cabins are arranged to assure privacy; you can sit on your covered porch and see nothing but the water, hear nothing but the call of the loons. In the lodge, you can prop your feet on the raised hearth of the huge circular fireplace and read or chat or nap.

The Mornings

Each morning Gus or Tim brings coffee or tea to your cabin, a gesture that ensures everyone makes it to breakfast. Janet and Leni prepare tasty and varied meals, served ranch style with more than enough for everyone at the table. Over sausages, hotcakes and hash browns, everyone decides on the day's fishing spot. Large lunches are already packed. Four-wheel drive vehicles are ready for you to take to one of the outlying lakes, where you'll find sturdy wooden boats equipped with outboard motors, boat cushions, anchors, nets and tackle boxes. Gus and Tim point you in the right direction, from there, it's up to you. Choose a different lake each day of your stay.

Cooperative Trout

The eight lakes provide plenty of variety, and only guests at the resort have access to them. Jerry and Rouse lakes are the most remote, perhaps the most scenic, and often yield the most fish. Fishing is consistently good. Because of the abundance of feed in these cold, spring-fed lakes, the trout commonly reach one to three pounds, and there is the opportunity to catch trophy fish. The fish aren't finicky either; just about any fishing method results in a good catch. Gus and Tim can't recall anyone who left empty-handed.

Seldom do non-fishermen feel left out; guests can follow their own paths, content with the absence of pressure, of responsibility, of things that must be done. Hatheume has a fleet of mountain bikes available for day or evening rides or for working off a hefty meal.

At the end of the day guests gather together again for dinner. It might be ribs or roast, veal cutlets or turkey, served with heaping plates of fresh vegetables and freshly baked rolls. Everything, including dessert, is as hearty as it is delicious. Evenings are peaceful and sleep comes easily.

Making Plans

This is a destination resort, so a holiday here requires thoughtful planning. Write early, ask questions, make your reservations. You need to remember that even during the hot summer months the temperature at this altitude (4,600 feet) can be brisk at night. Come prepared for the odd rain storm.

The main lodge and cabins face Hatheume Lake.

Most guests return again and again because they can depend on the hosts to be as cooperative as the fish. When your stay has ended, you may be reticent about packing your gear and starting your car again. Just take your fish (which can be frozen or smoked for your convenience), your photos, your memories and begin thinking about next year.

Getting There

From Vancouver, take Highway 1 eastward to Hope, then the new toll Coquihalla Highway 5 north to Merritt. Just outside Merritt exit right onto Highway 5A to Quilchena. About one-half mile beyond historic Quilchena Hotel, turn right onto a gravel road marked Pennask Lake and follow Hatheume signs to the resort for about two hours. Or, travel Highway 97 to Peachland. At the stoplight turn west to Brenda Mine (approximately sixteen miles). As you approach the mine turn left on a gravel road and follow signs for about twenty miles to Hatheume Lake. Allow a couple of hours for a leisurely drive to the lodge.

EMERALD LAKE RESORT

Address: P.O. Box 10, Field, British Columbia Canada V0A 1G0
Telephone: (604) 343-6321
    (800) 663-6336, reservations only
Host: Paul Holscher, Resident Manager
Room Rates: Superior rooms: low season, $95; regular season, $125; high season, $190. Deluxe rooms: low season, $120; regular season, $150; high season, $225. Executive suites: low season, $145; regular season, $180; high season, $250. (Canadian)
Credit Cards: American Express, EnRoute, MasterCard, Visa
Remarks: Children under 12 free with parents. No pets.

When he first spotted the lake, Tom Wilson knew he'd made a mistake, and an embarrassing one at that. As a guide working for the railroad in the late 1800's, Tom had come upon many an undiscovered lake and had aptly named them. But this one, was extraordinary. Encircled by a forest of giant pines, it had water as pure and tranquil as fine glacial silt, as sparkling green as an emerald. Emeralds! Emerald Lake.

But there already *was* an Emerald Lake. Tom had named it himself not long before. That had been a pretty lake, but nothing compared to this. "Perhaps Louise would fancy a lake being named after her," he thought.

Legend of a Bungalow Queen

Built by the Canadian Pacific Railway in 1902 as one of a series of bungalow camps erected to encourage travel and thus recoup the cost of the expensive rail line, the Emerald Lake Chalet was the creme de la creme. The majestic lodge of handhewn timber and massive stone fireplaces offered the very latest in modern conveniences – electricity, wood stoves, and hardwood floors. The rate even with the added amenity of a full orchestra to entertain the guests, was still exorbitant – $5 per day. The chalet became the private retreat only of the adventurous of spirit and the affluent.

Calgary resident Pat O'Connor had watched the sun set on the grandeur of the Emerald Lake Chalet many times. He was concerned over the steady decline of the chalet.

In 1980 Pat purchased the chalet and its surrounding thirteen acres, beginning a process, he recalls, that "I would never have dreamed could be so

difficult." The property, which was and continues to be under the scrutiny of Park Canada, took six years to restore.

Beautiful Balance

The $8.5 million renovation that produced the new Emerald Lake Lodge reflects O'Connor's respect for the delicate balance between commercial and environmental concerns. The 15,000 square foot chalet was restored to its rustic grandeur. The building's two massive stone fireplaces remain the focal point for the Emerald Lounge and lobby. And the Kicking Horse Bar's 1882 oak bar adds a grand reminder of the Yukon's lively Gold Rush days.

An old-fashioned veranda shades the new dining room's spectacular views. Elegant in chintzes of dusty rose, gray and hunter green, the rustic room has a comfortable coziness. And the menu's mountain cuisine successfully pleases nouvelle palates, as well as those that prefer simpler fare. But whatever your choice, leave room for dessert. The Chocolatissimo and Black Forest cakes, the blueberry, raspberry and strawberry cheesecakes and the assortment of fresh mousses are as spectacular as the lake itself.

The lodge's twenty-four new buildings were built twenty-five feet off the ground so that the surrounding vegetation would be able to regenerate. The 85 guest units spread over three hillsides. The studios and the suites contain queen size beds covered with comforters, and the homey feel of antiques and wicker. All rooms have stone hearth fireplaces (and an on call woodsman to light it for you), stocked mini-bars, private entrances, full baths and telephones. You won't find televisions, radios or clocks to distract you here.

Combining Business and Pleasure

An ideal location for board meetings, workshops and classroom-style seminars for 10 to 100, Emerald Lake Lodge offers seven conference areas and a full spectrum of audio-visual equipment. The lodge is especially suited to occasions such as weddings and anniversaries. Honeymoon units are set at the secluded end of the property and are thoughtfully stocked with chilled champagne, a floral bouquet and basket of assorted goodies.

There's a Club House with an outdoor 14-foot hot tub, sauna, sundeck and exercise room. The Day Lodge allows day-use visitors to relax on a sundeck, browse through the gift shop and enjoy the self-service restaurant.

Rare Spirit of the Canadian Rockies

"We're looking for people who want to spend time in the mountains, for people who want all the advantages of the Rockies without roughing it," says Pat. Emerald Lake Lodge does its best to fulfill the promise of the great outdoors.

This fireplace is in the 1903 Main Lodge.

The tour desk has ample information on such seasonal activities as horseback riding, canoeing, fishing, whitewater rafting and sightseeing. And while a car is best for getting to Takkakkaw Falls, the third tallest waterfall in Canada, a strenuous but rewarding two-hour hike will put you in the famous Burgess fossil beds. For ambitious hikers who want to wander the surrounding ranges, the lodge staff will arrange an overnight stay at hiking huts.

In the winter, you can ski the way Canadians prefer, from a helicopter. The area boasts some of the best heli-skiing in the world. For Nordic enthusiasts there are 50 miles of trails, where deer, elk and other wildlife roam. Or you can take a dog sled ride, try snow shoeing, or indulge in a moonlit sleigh ride.

Getting There

The lodge is six miles off the TransCanada Highway, and a two and one-half hour drive from Calgary and an hour from Banff. Rail service is available to the Field station, seven miles from the lodge. Guests are brought in by shuttle bus from the parking lot five minutes away.

BUFFALO MOUNTAIN LODGE

Address:	P.O. Box 1326, Banff, Alberta Canada TOL OCO
Telephone:	(403) 762-2400
	(800) 661-1367, reservations only
Host:	Paula Mattison, Resident Manager
Room Rates:	Deluxe and studio suites: low season, $90; regular season, $110; high season, $150. One-bedroom loft and two-bedroom chalets: low season, $120; regular season, $140; high season, $160. (Canadian)
Credit Cards:	American Express, EnRoute, MasterCard, Visa
Remarks:	No pets.

As the sun sank in the sky, Grey Hawk, a Blackfoot warrior started out of the valley. He paused, then turned back to the mountain, now bathed in twilight. The hunt had been successful, and slowly, solemnly, Grey Hawk danced and chanted a song in honor of Sleeping Buffalo, the symbol of the great beast of his tribe's survival.

The legend describes an area known today as Tunnel Mountain, overlooking scenic, historic Banff. The natives who first made this area their home both rejoiced in and respected its beauty and abundance. Bordered by the granite spires of Cascade Mountain and Mount Rundle, rock formations called hoodoos rose out of the sweeping Bow Valley, where moose, elk, deer and bison were plentiful, and the earth's hot mineral baths rejuvenation. It was a peaceful life for the Indians, a life of ceremony and celebration.

Respect For The Past

With a spirit of veneration for the past, for unspoiled nature and life's simple pleasures, Pat O'Connor and Canadian Rocky Mountain Resorts have transformed Mountview Village into Buffalo Mountain Lodge. On the outskirts of Banff, with panoramic views of the town, the Lodge's forested setting offers seclusion, privacy and pure mountain air. It's the kind of place that compels you to slow down.

"We were drawing from the past for things built properly and built with heart," says Witold Twardowski, the creative director of the Lodge. The love and craftsmanship that went into the Main Lodge's handhewn construction is evident. High, open-beamed ceilings display a massive stone fireplace and the custom made cherry, pine and bent-willow furnishings are beautifully accented with copper.

The simple elegance of the Lodge's design extends to the custom cherry and pine furnishings of the dining room. The Lodge's chefs, taking pride in using only the freshest ingredients, present delicious menus that feature hearty soups and breads, superb entrees and freshly baked pastries and desserts. In the summer, you can sample the cuisine from the shade of a patio table, or, at any time, enjoy breakfast in bed.

Legendary Hospitality

The 85 townhouse units spread across the property can accommodate up to 250 guests in two- and four-unit condominium-style buildings. You have the option of choosing from a deluxe unit with one queen bed or two double beds, or, for larger families a two-bedroom chalet that can sleep six and includes a full kitchen.

Throughout the units, the warm, rich tones of custom pine, antique and wicker furnishings are accented with splashes of turquoise and fresh floral arrangements. Most units included a stone fireplace and private balcony and all provide telephones, cable television and other personal touches.

True to its heritage as a Native gathering place, Buffalo Mountain Lodge is also a splendid meeting place. Two well-appointed conference rooms can accommodate from 20 to 200 people for seminars, workshops and retreats. One room features a balcony that commands a breathtaking view of Cascade Mountain, the second has a landscaped outdoor patio.

The Lodge's cheerful, professional staff go out of their way to pamper and please. Guests have access to the property's outdoor spa facilities, which include a sauna, oversized 14-foot hot tub and exercise room. A seasonal program of activities is available and you'll find all kinds of willing assistance in coordinating your wedding, dinner party or family reunion.

Tradition of a Rocky Mountain Holiday

No matter the season, Buffalo Mountain Lodge offers outdoor activities by day and the luxury of an Alpine resort by night. Banff, known the world over for its beauty and soothing hot mineral springs, provides the perfect base camp for exploring the outlying areas.

You can explore hiking trails by foot or by horseback, canoe or kayak down the beautiful Bow River. There's great golf at nearby Banff Springs, and the Lodge can provide picnic lunches for a day of fishing at Lake Minnewanka.

And the snow! Everyone's heard of the featherlight powder of the Canadian Rockies. With Banff's central location, you are close to four world-class ski mountains – Lake Louise, Mount Norquay, Sunshine and Nakiska. Take off on a pair of cross country skis to experience the thrill of untracked powder.

Custom pine, antique and wicker furnishings are in every room.

A variety of exciting ski packages, including heli-skiing, are available through the Lodge and Banff offers plenty of apres-ski night life.

Banff is also recognized for the excellence of Banff Centre's music, theatre and dance performances. The town tempts you with little boutiques, galleries and cafes. The Whyte Museum of the Canadian Rockies and the Luxton Museum do an outstanding job of reproducing the colorful history of Banff National park and its Native people.

Banff is best appreciated during the less crowded months. The fall and spring are ideal times to visit without the crowds associated with the busier summer and winter.

Getting There

Buffalo Mountain Lodge is located on Tunnel Mountain Road in Banff just off the TransCanada Highway. The Calgary International Airport is one and one-half hours away. Passenger rail and bus service is also available to Banff.

Northern
Rockies

The Northern Rockies is an incredible region. The states of Idaho, Montana, Wyoming and Utah are big, high, dry and lonely.

This vast region is sparsely populated (only three in 100 Americans live here), and has an average of just 14" of rain a year. The dominant geological feature is the strong spine of mountains that form the backbone of the area and define its open and lonely spaces.

Idaho

Idaho is river country, with over 16,000 miles of rivers and 2,000 lakes. The Snake, Salmon (The River of No-Return), Clearwater and Middlefork are but a few of the thousands of watery fingers scratching the state's spiny back. The Snake is the sixth longest river in the U.S. and drains an area as big as New York and New England combined. It has created North America's deepest gorge, Hells Canyon at 9,300 feet.

The Sawtooth and White Cloud Mountains north of Sun Valley are some of the most spectacular anywhere. A few hours south is an 80 square mile area where, thousands of years ago, melted rock poured out of great cracks and flowed across the land. Walking in The Craters of the Moon National Monument, it's easy to feel that you're on another planet.

Montana

The sheer size of Montana is impressive. The nation's fourth largest state, it spans 550 miles in length by about half that in width. If placed along the Atlantic seacoast, it would stretch from Boston to Richmond, Virginia.

Montana is home to both Glacier and Yellowstone National Parks. Glacier, in the northwestern corner, is a masterwork of 50 glaciers and over 200 sparkling lakes. Not to be missed is the Going-to-the-Sun Road that cuts a 50-mile path east to west across the Continental Divide.

Flathead Lake is the largest freshwater lake in the west. Within its 200 square miles is an island state park containing Bighorn sheep.

Wyoming

Wyoming has two nicknames, the Cowboy State and the Equality State. Before its admittance to statehood the territory granted women the rights to vote and hold public office. There may have been an ulterior motive in this 1869 burst of equality. Back then the ratio was six men for every woman. The vote was seen as a smart move to entice women into the territory. It must have worked, and soon women were not only voting but holding office, too. Wyoming had the first woman justice of the peace, superintendent of schools, state representative and, in 1924, the first woman governor.

It is now clear that, in spite of the 1988 fires, Yellowstone will always remain one of the most unique places in the world. Yellowstone is shared by both Montana and Wyoming and is America's first and most famous National Park. It is one of the great wildlife sanctuaries. Bald eagles soar and the once nearly-extinct Trumpeter Swan peacefully glides across calm lakes. Grizzlies, moose and elk share the park with buffalo and many other species.

Just below the southern gate to Yellowstone is a fifty-five mile long valley completely surrounded by five mountain ranges. This is the valley of Jackson Hole. On the west is one of the world's most spectacular ranges of all, rising 7,400 from the nearly treeless valley, the Grand Tetons.

The French explorers, impressed with the mountains' size and jagged peaks, gave them this well deserved name. The Tetons are a slab of rock titled upward along a fault line. This started ten million years ago and continues at a rate of about one foot every three hundred years. The range stands out from the rest of the sixty-five million year old Rockies since it is so young and jagged.

Jackson, the gateway to both Yellowstone and Grand Teton National Parks, has roots in the early 1800's when the fur trappers arrived. In the Old West, the streets were often thick with mud, and the mark of a civilized town was having wooden sidewalks. Those sidewalks are still in use in Jackson and the town is still considered very civilized . It's art and cultural activities have earned it the title of "Santa Fe of the Rockies."

Utah

Utah is an intriguing state. The state bird is a sea gull, even though the state lies more than 500 miles from the nearest ocean. Within the boundaries are five national parks, including parts of Dinosaur National Monument. In Arches National Park, Landscape Arch at 291 feet is the longest natural arch in America.

Most of the state's residents live in a 150 mile narrow fertile strip along the Wasatch Mountains where the original Mormons settled in 1847. Thousands of years ago a lake bigger than Lake Superior covered most of northwestern Utah. Driving along now you can see where the waves of ancient Lake Bonneville cut wide flat shorelines, called "terraces," along the mountains. Stone Age hunters lived in caves along the shore where modern homes are now being built.

The state and emotional capital is Salt Lake City. Wide streets and tree-lined sidewalks give the city an airy, open feeling. Twenty-seven miles east of the city via a scenic drive through Parley's Canyon is Park City, Utah's largest ski area. Receiving about 350 inches of snow annually, Park City is the home of the U.S. ski team and offers 82 runs and over 2,200 acres of skiable terrain.

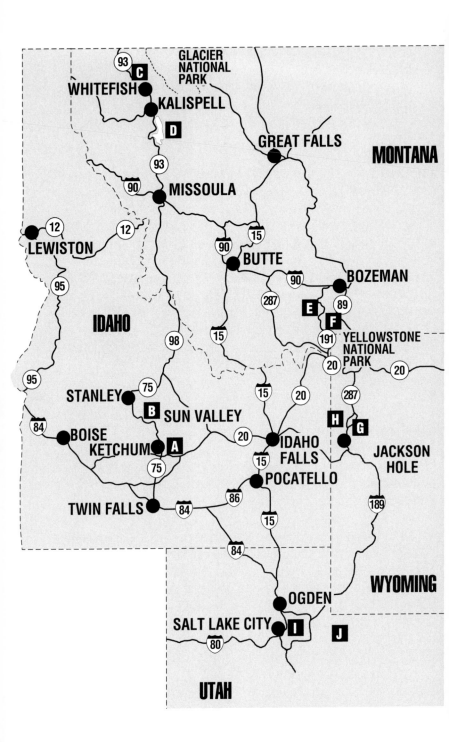

NORTHERN ROCKIES SPECIAL PLACES

A River Street Inn

B Busterback Ranch

C Kandahar Lodge

D Flathead Lake Lodge

E Lone Mountain Ranch

F Mountain Sky Ranch

G The Wort Hotel

H Spring Creek Resort

I The Brigham Street Inn

J The Homestead

RIVER STREET INN

Address:	100 Rivers Street West, Ketchum, ID 83340
	P.O. Box 182, Sun Valley, ID 83353
Telephone:	(208) 726-3611
Location:	On Trail Creek in south Ketchum
Hosts:	Ginny Van Doren, Bonnie Barclay
Room Rates:	$95 to $145 double. Single, Senior citizen,
	commercial and holiday rates are available.
Credit Cards:	American Express, Discover, MasterCard, Visa
Remarks:	No smoking in bedrooms.

Neatly tucked on a quiet street just a few blocks from the core of Ketchum, River Street Inn is a pleasing blend of friendly warmth and respectful privacy. Its innovative architecture melds the charm of turn-of-the-century Victorian sensibilities with the open, airy spaces of contemporary western design. Palladian windows, polished brass and whitewashed oak combine to create a soothing environment.

The spacious living room is dominated by a natural brick fireplace. The comfortable colors of the parlor seating—sage green, ivory and dusty rose —invite you to linger over a cup of tea.

From the living room, French doors open onto an expansive deck. Cotton-woods and aspens border Trail Creek which runs below. The deck provides an ideal spot for early morning bird watching or late night star gazing.

The eight guest rooms are really more like guest suites. Decorated in soft prints and pastels, they furnish queen-size beds, walk-in showers, small refrigerators, and Japanese soaking tubs, the perfect panacea for weary muscles. Five of the suites face the rocky tumble of Trail Creek. Its soothing symphony coaxes restful sleep. Three suites overlooking mountain vistas invite peaceful contemplation and relaxation. In the winter you can watch the weather on Bald Mountain, "Baldy," in order to best time your departure to the slopes for a day of skiing.

"No Rules" Rule

The intimate atmosphere of the inn was co-owner Ginny Van Doren's special goal. Years ago, Ginny left her job in San Francisco and found her heart in Sun Valley. Over the years, she honed her skills by working for several restaurants in the area. Her experience led to her own success formula, one which she and

THE
RIVER STREET INN
BED AND BREAKFAST

GINNY VANDOREN ✦ PROPRIETRESS

reservationist Bonnie Barclay share. River Street Inn's secret: let the guests set the tone. If you wish to visit over a cup of coffee in the kitchen, the more the merrier. However, if privacy is your goal, it is most assuredly respected. Ginny and Bonnie are available for friendly conversation or to assist in any arrangements or information you need to enhance your stay.

River Street Breakfast

Breakfast at River Street Inn is an indulgent feast which will carry you well through lunchtime. Begin with fresh fruits, juices, coffee or tea. Dive into one of Ginny's homemade baked Danish rolls or coffeecake. A special entrée, one of Ginny's surprise concoctions, follows: ricotta pancakes, frittatas, spinach and sausage puff pastry, or German apple pancakes are among her favorites. Ginny's "no rules" rule means breakfast may be eaten on your own schedule. As she says, "Breakfast is from 8 to 10, unless guests want it earlier or later, or in bed."

In winter, skiers gather for "après ski" in the inn's living room. The gathering is always friendly and relaxed. In summertime, iced tea is served on the deck overlooking the creek.

Down in the Valley

Ketchum and Sun Valley are situated in the narrow Wood River Valley. Sun Valley is most noted as a skiers haven. Imposing Bald Mountain hovers over the town. Baldy has 16 chair lifts and over 64 runs on its 3,400 feet of vertical drop. The area offers some of the most challenging skiing in the country, yet has appeal for skiers at all levels of expertise. Sun Valley's expert staff of ski instructors is nationally acclaimed. A free shuttle runs from just across the street from River Street Inn to the base of River Run. Nordic skiing is popular in the valley, and local outfitters will arrange backcountry trips for skiers in search of unbroken powder.

Summer and Fall

Summer and fall visitors have the opportunity to see yet another side of Sun Valley's personality. The high desert climate is warm, dry and dependable. The fall is a patchwork of colors as aspen trees go through their yearly changes. A full line-up of sports are available including horseback riding, bicycling and hiking. Four golf courses in the valley entice expert and duffer alike. There are special guest privileges at the million dollar athletic club just one-half block away as well. A view of the valley is best seen by hot air balloon or the Hailey Airport gliders. Just south of Hailey, Magic Reservoir awaits waterskiers and windsurfers alike.

Wood River Valley is also home to some of the best trout fishing streams in the country. Ketchum's many fine shops entice shoppers who browse for

All rooms have a queen-size bed, refrigerator and a Japanese soaking tub.

year-round sport clothing as well as furs and leather goods. The town offers many fine art galleries and restaurants with selections ranging from natural foods to elegant Basque or French cuisine.

North of Ketchum is a cemetery where a simple slab marks Ernest Hemingway's grave. Farther out on Trail Creek, in the heart of the country he called home, you'll find the Hemingway memorial. On it is written: "Best of all he loved the fall... the leaves yellow on the cottonwoods, leaves floating on the trout streams and above the hills the high blue windless skies."

Getting There

Fly into Hailey Airport, south of Ketchum, and take a taxi or rental car to the inn. Heading north on U.S. 75, turn left at River Street, just beyond the Trail Creek Bridge. The inn is two blocks toward the mountains, on your left. There is plenty of private parking in front of the inn.

BUSTERBACK RANCH

Address:	Star Route, Ketchum, ID 83340
Telephone:	(208) 774-2217
Location:	Forty miles north of Ketchum on State Highway 75
Host:	Jim Root, Managing Director
Room Rates:	Winter: $135.00 per person a day
	Summer: $115.00 per person a day
	Off Season: $95.00 a couple, includes breakfast
Credit Cards:	MasterCard, Visa
Remarks:	Winter rates include three family style creative meals, ski equipment, lesson and use of the trails. Summer includes meals and use of the mountain bikes, windsurfers and canoe. Off Season includes lodging and whatever recreation the weather allows.

Busterback Ranch is a year-round resort and working cattle ranch 40 miles north of Sun Valley. Like a pearl in a jagged oyster shell, Busterback rests in Idaho's Stanley Basin between the Sawtooth and White Cloud Mountain ranges. Its eastern boundary is the Salmon River, otherwise known as the River of No Return.

"John Breckenridge owned the ranch just before I did," owner Dr. Lee Enright explained. "His father homesteaded the place in 1910 and sort of carved the ranch out of the sagebrush. Breckenridge had a small cabin over by Petit Lake and his wife used to say 'If you keep coming up here and workin' so hard you're going to bust yer back.'" Well, the name stuck, and eventually the main ranch was known as Busterback. For today's guest, however, life is anything *but* bust yer back.

Mountain Mecca

Busterback's assemblage of log buildings is a mecca in the broad Stanley Basin. Situated on 2,800 acres, it commands a view of the entire valley. A main lodge houses the community living area, a kitchen and five guest rooms. At night it glows with candlelight and warmth from a cheery fireplace. The living room is comfortably decorated with oak chests, plush sofas a picture window with a view of the Sawtooths. Near the etched front door of the ranch house, a hand written scroll depicts the history of Busterback Ranch.

Each of the ranch house bedrooms is individually appointed with Indian rugs, western prints, peeled log furniture and brass fixtures, thick comforters and

crisp linens. Lace ruffles adorn the queen and twin beds. Two rooms offer private baths; three share. Three neat log cabins, Alpine, Alturas and Toxaway, sit just off the main house and offer quality, secluded accommodations. The Western motif continues here in the woodman's plaid comforters, peeled log furniture and wood burning stoves.

Adjoining the main house is the recently added White Cloud Lodge. With its tall, stone fireplace and long dining table, this comfortable room accommodates Busterback's day visitors. Overnight guests can also enjoy mingling here, yet retain the privacy of the main lodge. The ranch house is rimmed by a large sun deck, an ideal spot for viewing the vast valley and sunbathing in Idaho's bold sun.

Guests dine family style around the kitchen's butcher block table. Bountiful breakfast spreads feature omelettes bubbling with cheese, ranch potatoes, egg quesadillas or orange pancakes. Fresh ground coffee, juices and fruits accompany the meal. There are a selection of homemade soups and delicious cookies for lunch. Dinners feature an exotic feast of delicacies created by Busterback's culinary wizards. Roast Idaho Rack of Lamb, Pork Tenderloins in Red Chile Pepper Glaze, California Seafood Stew and Chicken Breasts with Tequila and Lime are a few of the entrées. Leafy salads, saffron rice or Idaho spuds are added to make a colorful table. A fine selection of wines, beers and liquors complement the meal. Scrumptious desserts follow, such as Roaring Meg's Chocolate Cake, Poached Pears or Homemade Cheese Cakes with Fresh Fruit, so be sure to save room.

An aura of comraderie prevails as guests gather in the living room after dinner. The evening may close with a gentle walk, a quiet view of a spectacular sunset, or a seasonal meteor shower.

Big Valley

The valley offers a spectrum of activities appealing to all levels of interests and abilities year-round. From the first snowfall through late spring, Busterback maintains 56 kilometers of meticulously groomed trails which begin just outside the back door. The trails vary in difficulty and length, so novice and expert alike are satisfied. Busterback's staff of fully qualified instructors are on hand to give lessons and pointers. A gear room stocks equipment in all sizes. Ski to one of the nearby lakes and drop into the 70-year-old sheepherder's wagon, now a warming hut, for a cup of tea. A local outfitter will arrange back country ski trips into the Sawtooth or White Cloud Mountains for day treks or overnight stays in a Mongolian style yurt.

Cross the Galena Summit to reach the world famous ski area of Sun Valley. Abundant Rocky Mountain powder snow falls here to make one of the country's finest downhill skiing areas. Novice and expert skiers choose from a broad selection of slopes. Instruction and equipment rentals are available.

The White Cloud Lodge adjoins the main lodge.

Busterback's summertime complexion is that of an actual working cattle ranch. Two thousand head of cattle share the acreage. Guests are invited to watch the cowboys in action, but Busterback is not a "dude ranch," so joining in is not part of the curriculum. Horses are available for day trips into the Sawtooth National Recreation Area.

Float trips on the Salmon River are a favorite with summer guests, as are hiking, fishing and mountain bike rides. Busterback has canoes and windsurfers. Summer rates include use of windsurfers, canoe and mountain bikes. Horseback riding and haywagon rides are available for additional charge. After a full day of adventure you can return to Busterback for a hearty meal, a soak in the hot tub, or a bake in the Finnish sauna.

Getting There

Drive forty miles north from Ketchum and Sun Valley on State Highway 75, crossing Galena Summit. Approximately six miles from the base of the mountain, watch for signs and turn right into the Busterback driveway.

KANDAHAR LODGE

Address:	Big Mountain Ski Resort Village, P.O. Box 1659, Whitefish, MT 59937
Telephone:	(406) 862-6098
Location:	On Big Mountain, eight miles north of Whitefish
Hosts:	Buck and Mary Pat Love
Room Rates:	$50 single, $64 double, $98 suites (summer); $74 to $134 rooms, $106 to $158 lofts, $180 two-room suites (winter). Weekly rates, season packages and one-bedroom apartment are also available.
Credit Cards:	American Express, MasterCard, Visa
Remarks:	Children under 12 stay free.

Kandahar, the story goes, is an obscure town in Afghanistan that was, in August 1880, the location of a besieged British garrison. British General Frederick Roberts marched to their rescue with 10,000 troops. He was knighted for his efforts and took the name Lord Roberts of Kandahar. Years later, as the vice president of an alpine sports club, Roberts lent his name to the trophy awarded the champion of the downhill racing event, and the Roberts of Kandahar Challenge Cup led to the creation of the Kandahar Ski Club, which sponsored the first international ski meet in which the winner is chosen on the basis of combined downhill and slalom race scores.

And so it came to pass that Buck and Mary Pat Love, two ski devotees with an admiration for the grand style of European ski lodges, named the alpine ski lodge in Whitefish, Montana, "Kandahar."

European Style Lodge

Mary Pat and Buck wanted to create an entire package: great skiing, beautiful scenery, and first class lodging and dining. From the start, they decided their priority was to spend as much time as possible with guests, to concentrate on making visitors feel at home and comfortable. They built their home as part of the lodge and are, in the best sense of the word, innkeepers.

Their "inn" is a three story European style lodge built around a central sunken lobby with an immense rock fireplace, an array of comfortable sofas and chairs flanked by reading lamps, a big screen VHS and upright piano. The walls are sided with knotty cedar and massive support beams. The entrance to the lodge has window arches and side panels of etched glass that display mountain and forest scenes by local Whitefish artist Myni Ferguson. On either side of the lobby, wide staircases lead guests to their second- and third-floor rooms, suites or lofts. Guests can reserve accommodations for one to

eight people. Sixteen of the 48 units have small fully stocked kitchens. Enough kitchenware to cook a Thanksgiving dinner is provided, or the space can be used simply for storing drinks and snacks. The rooms have the same cedar paneling, sand colored carpets and color photos of skiing and sailing that decorate the lobby.

Skiers who return from the slopes of Big Mountain can ski right up to the front door of Kandahar, enter a heated boot room to remove ski gear, and walk in stocking feet to one of the two saunas, or to the jacuzzis for a long, slow dip into the 102° water.

Cafe Kandahar

After a Continental dinner in the Cafe Kandahar (specialties include sauerbraten mit katoffelklossen, chicken Maria, coquille St. Jacques and flounder Florentine), skiers and nonskiers alike can relax in the small lounge opposite the lobby, watch television, play cribbage or any of a number of board and card games. The lounge does not sell liquor, however, guests are welcome to bring their own in for consumption during the meal.

Year-Round Enjoyment

Kandahar Lodge is open year-round and offers guests an assortment of activities. In the summer season (May to October), visitors can make the cool mountain resort their home base and take day trips to majestic Glacier National Park, the rugged Mission Mountains, the astonishingly blue Flathead Lake, and the nearby towns of Whitefish and Kalispell. For the outdoor enthusiast, there is bicycling, camping, boating and waterskiing, fishing, float trips, golf, hiking, hunting and windsurfing.

In April, the North American Ski/Yachting Championships take place on Big Mountain and Flathead Lake. For sailors who ski and skiers who sail, this event provides the perfect combination of mountain skiing and sailing on the nearly frozen waters of Flathead.

In the winter months (November to April), Big Mountain and the Kandahar Lodge are blanketed with fresh, powdery snow, so there is plenty of wintertime fun, too. Eagle watchers flock to West Glacier to catch sight of the showy birds in October and November; Whitefish holds its annual Winter Carnival in early February; and snow lovers ride sleighs and chair lifts to pursue their sports. Cross-country skiers have miles of trails and roads to glide over, too.

One of the Best

Ski magazine called 6,770-foot Big Mountain "one of the best ski areas in the world." With 33 miles of ski terrain, 41 different runs and a daily skier capacity of 6,000, this claim is hard to dispute. They are opening up the back side of

The lobby is a very comfortable place to gather and relax.

the mountain for skiing in areas not previously used. There are five lifts, a T-bar, a platter lift and a new Quad lift. Daytime tickets cost $14 to $25; night skiing tickets (there are 53 acres of lighted runs) are $9. Private lessons are available from the Big Mountain Ski School. Children under 6 ski free.

The winter's crisp air on Big Mountain carries the clean scent of evergreens, and the view of the Flathead Valley is stunning. The practically nonexistent lift lines, even during the Christmas and New Year's, mean that Kandahar's guests can ski to their hearts' content.

Getting There

Highway 93 North takes you alongside Flathead Lake through Kalispell and into Whitefish. In Whitefish, turn right onto Wisconsin Avenue (Highway 487) and follow the signs to Big Mountain. Kandahar Lodge is about eight miles north of Whitefish. Amtrak takes train travelers to the Whitefish depot, and buses and taxis ferry passengers to the mountaintop. Delta and Horizon airlines have daily flights just 45 minutes from the Lodge.

FLATHEAD LAKE LODGE

Address:	P.O. Box 248, Bigfork, MT 59911
Telephone:	(406) 837-4391
Location:	Highway 35, one mile south of Bigfork
Hosts:	Doug and Maureen Averill
Rates:	Adults $989, teenagers $797, children from four to 12 $671, children under four $96, single occupancy $1078. Rates Sunday to Sunday.
Credit Cards:	None. Personal checks accepted.
Remarks:	No pets. Open May through September. Reservations required.

The Averill family's Flathead Lake Lodge and Dude Ranch offers guests one full week of lodging, meals and recreational activities on their 2,000-acre ranch on the east shore of Flathead Lake, and has been doing so since 1945. The lodge caters to families with children of all ages, and the 100 guests are limited only by their inability to do everything at once. *Sunset, Better Homes and Gardens* and *Travel and Leisure* have all featured the lodge for providing one of the finest family vacations in America.

The Wranglers

"People come here for the horses," says Doug Averill, an ex-rodeo rider who became manager of the ranch when his dad, Les Averill, retired in 1975. "We have dude horses for the inexperienced riders and quality quarterhorses for those who know how to handle that kind of horse. A lot of the people are simply nuts about horses." And so the Averills give them horses morning, noon and night. Guests can sign up for breakfast rides, group rides, and family rides or fast rides. The wranglers start their day at 5:30, but even at that hour there are kids down at the stable to help them brush and feed the horses.

At the end of the week, there is a kid's rodeo, and children of all ages participate in the barrel races, pole bending contests, three-legged races and the water balloon challenge. "The rodeo is for fun. It's not meant to be competitive," Doug explains. Once a week, a roping club comes to the ranch to put on a performance, and Buck, a longtime ranch hand, entertains guests with stories and demonstrations of old-time skills such as braiding rope.

On Flathead Lake

As much as guests love the horses, it would be impossible to forget the lake. The clear blue waters of Flathead lap at the shore of the ranch, and guests are encouraged to take out the sailboats, fishing boats, canoes and windsurfers

at any time. There's waterskiing everyday at one o'clock, and an experienced waterfront hand (referred to as a water wimp by the wranglers) is nearby to handle the powerboat and give lessons.

For those who prefer the moving water of a river, Flathead Lake Lodge offers raft trips and inner tube floats on the Swan and Flathead rivers. For even more excitement, guests can go white water rafting or take a raft fishing trip.

If the horses and the lake don't take up all the free time a guest has, he or she can play tennis, volleyball or basketball, swim in the lake or pool, attend the nightly beach fires and sing-alongs, work in the ranch's vegetable and flower garden, take a day trip to Glacier National Park, or just sit on one of the dozens of benches, chairs or lounges that are spread around the ranch. The game room appeals to kids from three to 30, and a game room monitor takes kids on nature hikes to gather the raw materials for future projects: painted rock people and pinecone cowboys.

There are, in fact, only two things that guests can't do: they can't watch television and they can't play video games. There aren't any in the cabins or the lodges.

The Lodge

The Civilian Conservation Corps built the Main Lodge and the South Lodge in 1932, and both two-story Western structures have large lobbies with huge river rock fireplaces. The walls and floors are constructed of larch, and so are the tables and chairs. The Main Lodge houses the office, Saddle Sore Saloon (guests bring their own liquor), kitchen and family style dining room, a few rooms for single guests and quarters for the kitchen staff. The walls of the lobby are decorated with trophies of past hunting expeditions: bear, moose, elk, deer, bighorn sheep, antelope, mountain goat and buffalo. The 25 to 30 families that arrive at the ranch each Sunday are housed in 17 cottages and cabins, constructed in the 1940s and '50s, that accommodate four to six people. Each unit has its own bath, two or three bedrooms, a comfortable living room and Western furnishings. Other outbuildings contain the game room, laundry, wood shop and horses' tack room and stables.

Family Style Dining

The lodge and dude ranch are completely self-sustaining. The kitchen staff bakes the bread, plans the desserts and prepares all the meals. Breakfast might consist of huckleberry pancakes and bacon and eggs one day and omelettes the next. Coffee is always served first thing in the morning, for the Averills know that many adults enjoy that first cup while standing next to a crackling fire in the Main Lodge. Lunch is light: salads and quiche or the food that kids like — hamburgers and soups. If the weather cooperates, and it usually does in the summer, lunch is served outside on the deck overlooking

244

The main lodge built in 1932 faces Flathead Lake.

the lake. Dinner might be a steak fry, fresh salmon, chicken, prime rib or a whole pig.

The unique combination of the lodge, its setting and recreational activities give the Averills an almost unheard-of repeat rate. Over 70 percent of Flathead Lake Lodge's guests come back again. Many come every other year, like one German family who has made the trip seven times. Mr. George Wood holds the record: he has come every summer for the last 37 years. It all started with his honeymoon... George and his wife never missed the first two weeks of August on the lake. George became known as Grandpa George and even gave Maureen Averill, Doug's wife, away on her wedding day.

Getting There

From Polson, follow Highway 35 north along the east side of Flathead Lake. The sign for the ranch is about one mile south of Bigfork. From Glacier National park, take Highway 40 toward Columbia Falls, turn onto 206, heading south. It will join with Highway 35, which will lead you past Bigfork and one mile south to the ranch.

■ LONE MOUNTAIN RANCH

Address:	P.O. Box 69, Big Sky, Montana 59716
Telephone:	(406) 995-4644
Location:	Four and one-half miles off Highway 191
Hosts:	Bob and Vivian Schaap and Mike Ankeny
Rates:	$725 per person per week, double. Includes three meals a day, airport transportation and a wide variety of recreational activities. Reduced rates for families with children.
Credit Cards:	MasterCard, Visa
Remarks:	Open June to October; December to April. Reservations required. No pets.

Nestled in its own secluded valley next to a clear mountain stream, Lone Mountain Ranch is a dream destination for lovers of the outdoors. Summer family fun, spectacular fly fishing, horseback riding and nordic skiing adventures are all packaged to include comfortable Western lodging and ranch meals in a friendly, informal atmosphere. With its close proximity (twenty miles) to the natural wonders of Yellowstone National Park, Lone Mountain Ranch provides guests with enough activities to keep them actively happy for way longer than a week's visit allows.

■ Yellowstone City

The ranch house was built in 1915 from hand-hewed logs. Originally a working cattle operation, Bob and Vivian Schaap took it over in 1977 to create a cross-country ski center and summer guest ranch. The 20 immaculate cabins accommodate guests—couples to large families—with all the comforts of home: cozy fireplaces, electric heat, private baths, and even front porches. The cabins are decorated with Indian artifacts. And each possesses its own unique character. Guests have been known to reserve the same special cabin year after year. With the ranch's excellent airline access, great snow and magnificent surroundings, it's not hard to understand why the Schaaps and their partner, Mike Ankeny, think they are "lucky to live in just about the prettiest spot on Earth!"

■ Ranch Cooking with Gourmet Flair

An active day at the ranch will certainly build hearty appetites. The dinner bell is always a welcome sound. Guests are treated to gourmet ranch cuisine served in traditional family style—lots of food on big platters. Three abundant meals are presented daily in the relaxed atmosphere of the ranch's beautiful new dining room. Delicious sack lunches are prepared for guests who choose to be out and about at lunchtime. In the summer, there are special weekly

dinners scheduled: a dinner horse ride, steak barbecue, a campfire sing-along, and a Saturday morning breakfast cookout. The ranch is always willing to accommodate vegetarian and special diets.

Summer Family Fun

The ranch successfully integrates activities for guests of all ages. Children can choose from a variety of fun adventures including campouts in an authentic teepee, horseback rides, rodeos, nature walks, and cooking pizza in a century-old woodburning cook stove. Little ones are supervised at the Lodgepole playground, and babysitting is available a few afternoons a week. Guests often bring along a friend or relative to assist with child care.

Horseback trips are a favorite activity for adults, too. Sunday is reserved for fitting guests with horses and tack. Monday through Saturday you can saddle up for a half-day ride to the Spanish Peaks, or an all-day trip into Yellowstone National Park. Wranglers accompany the small groups and are quick to point out the back country wildlife.

The ranch has an increasingly popular Naturalist program. Yellowstone interpretive trips offer guests opportunities to explore the Park's famous features as well as its well-kept secrets. Guided nature walks are available.

Guests can shake out their saddle sores by swing dancing to lively Western tunes or soaking in the hot tub under the big Montana sky. Evening entertainment may also include ballads of mountain man lore and grizzly bear tales accompanied by a Western guitar. The Horsefly Saloon is a comfortable spot to share adventure stories with other visitors.

Fly-fishing Paradise

Lone Mountain Ranch is paradise for the angler. The fly fishing program has qualified the ranch to be included on the Orvis-endorsed list. (Orvis is the oldest and largest fly fishing equipment manufacturer in the world.) Angling adventures can include wading, float-tubing or fishing from a drift boat. Fall is the perfect season to fish the nearby blue ribbon trout streams.

Winter Wonderland

Located right in the middle of deep powder snow country, the ranch is an ideal destination for a nordic winter holiday. Lone Mountain Ranch offers 45 miles of machine-tracked trails that begin right outside the cabin doors. First-track telemarking hounds can anticipate miles of back country blanketed by virgin snow. The ranch has a full-service ski shop, complete with rental and demo equipment. Professional instructors teach beginning fundamentals and also offer private workshops. All-day guided trips to Yellowstone and Spanish Peaks are available throughout the week. There is nothing that compares to

The winter snows bring "world class" cross country skiing.

the thrill of skiing through geyser basins, past snow-ghosted trees, frozen waterfalls, and wintering herds of elk and bison.

A highlight of the week, and a must on the "to do" list, is the evening sleigh ride up to the North Fork Cabin for a prime rib dinner.

Getting There

From the north, exit off Interstate 90 at Bozeman, Montana. Go south on Highway 191 to the Gallatin Canyon for forty miles. Turn right at the Big Sky Resort turnoff. Proceed up the Big Sky Spur Road four and one-half miles to the Lone Mountain Ranch sign. From Yellowstone, exit the West Entrance of the park to West Yellowstone. Drive forty-eight miles north on Highway 191 to the Big Sky Resort turnoff. Turn left and proceed as above.

MOUNTAIN SKY GUEST RANCH

Address:	Big Creek Road, Emigrant, MT, P.O. Box 1128, Bozeman, MT 59771 for reservations
Telephone:	(406) 587-1244, toll free (800) 548-3392
Location:	Four and one-half miles up Big Creek Road, off Highway 89 in south central Montana
Hosts:	Alan and Mary Brutger
Rates:	July and August: Adult single $1155-$1260, double $980-$1120. Children 7-12 $840-$980, six and under $525-$735.
Credit Cards:	Personal checks, MasterCard, VISA accepted.
Remarks:	No pets. Open May to October.

Nestled high in the Rocky Mountains, just 30 miles from Yellowstone National Park, is Mountain Sky Guest Ranch, one of the top-rated guest ranches in the Northern Rockies.

Mountain Sky was built in the mid-1930s—the old cabins, the lodge and their furniture were crafted with wood taken right off the property. The original cabins and split log furniture are still to be found at the ranch, however today they are blended with new furnishings to provide a cozy, serene setting for your family vacation.

Yellowstone City

"Yellowstone City," the main lodge, has three massive rock fireplaces, braided rugs over wooden floors and a piano, unlike any other, made from rough-hewn lodgepole pine. (You will also find a grand piano for the serious musicians.) The main lodge houses a comfortable great room, the kitchen, the lounge and bar, two dining rooms, a meeting room and the office.

"Cinnebar," like all the new cabins, has a spacious sitting room, wall-to-wall carpeting, comfortable furniture, a small refrigerator, coffeemaker, modern bath, generous closet space and a Montana-sized picture window that displays the surrounding mountains. The cabin sleeps two to four, and, most importantly, it is a place in which a family can feel at home.

"Black Pine" is an example of one of the old cabins that has been thoroughly remodeled to include modern conveniences without destroying the rustic ambiance. These one-, two- or three-bedroom cabins have a rock fireplace or wood burning stove and Western post-and-pole furniture, and can accommodate families large or small in comfort. All of the cabins at Mountain Sky,

new and old, have daily housekeeping, an inviting front porch with hanging flower baskets, and a basket of fresh fruit replenished daily. Guests may use telephones in the lodge but don't look for telephones or televisions in the cabins, because there aren't any.

Sunday to Sunday

The week at Mountain Sky begins on Sunday. Guests can use the afternoon to freshen up, unpack, walk down to the stables or tennis courts, or enjoy a complimentary drink poolside while getting to know their neighbors. After dinner, the staff makes its welcome and announces the week's schedule.

For horse lovers there are breakfast, morning and afternoon rides over miles of trails on the ranch and adjacent Gallatin National Forest. Riders can spot deer, elk, moose and if they are lucky black bear and possibly a mountain lion amid the rocky cliffs, grassy meadows and forested slopes of the ranch. The weeks riding activities culminate with a "showdeo" in which all guests are encouraged to show off their skills in events such as pole bending and egg on spoon races.

Fly-fishing is another major attraction at the ranch. Guests can practice their casting at the private trout pond or walk to Big Creek which borders the ranch for some excellent fishing. Nearby are the Yellowstone River, Nelson and Armstrong spring creeks, for world class trout fishing.

Guests can enjoy hiking, tennis on championship courts, or relaxing in the hot tub, heated pool or sauna. There is also volleyball, billiards, ping pong, horseshoes and an aerobics studio with professionally taught classes.

The evenings are capped off by a variety of entertainment. A typical week will include western dance instruction, a folk concert, dancing to a local combo and sing-a-longs at the piano led by staff or guests.

Vacation for All

Although this is a family oriented ranch, Alan Brutger and his staff know very well that parents need a vacation, too. For children of all ages, counselors supervise nature walks, swimming, games and fishing in a private trout pond. A Children's Wrangler gives guidance and instructions on horsemanship basics and special "Kids Dinners" are prepared after which activities such as a hayride, Indian pow wow or softball take place. This allows the adults to fully enjoy the gourmet cuisine found at Mountain Sky.

Mountain air and activity work up mighty appetites, and the ranch is well equipped to meet the challenge. The pastries, cinnamon rolls, croissants and muffins are freshly baked each morning and guests may choose from omelettes, ham and eggs, fresh fruit, granola or blueberry pancakes. Lunchtime

The historic barn and corrals are a short walk from the cabins.

offers a casual buffet, served outside, with a line-up of salads, soups and a hot specialty dish. Dinner is a gourmet affair with beef Wellington, poached salmon, veal medallion or rack of lamb as the main course.

Yellowstone National Park is about the only reason to leave Mountain Sky Ranch — its geysers, canyons, prairies, hot springs, lakes and wildlife are not to be missed. The park is a pleasurable day trip from the ranch. Picnic lunches and car pools are easily arranged.

Getting There

Turn off I-90 at Livingston, heading south on Highway 89 for thirty-nine miles. Look for the sign for Mountain Sky Guest Ranch at the Big Creek Road turn off. Be advised that the four and one-half miles to the ranch are slow. For travelers headed to the ranch from Yellowstone, the Mountain Sky turn off will be on the left-hand side of Highway 89, thirty miles north of Gardiner.

THE WORT HOTEL

Address:	P.O. Box 69, Jackson, WY 83001
Telephone:	(307) 733-2190, (800) 322-2727
Hosts:	Vernon Johnson, General Manager
	Carlene Barthel, Resident Manager
Room Rates:	Guest rooms: fall/spring, $70 to $80; winter, $85 to $95; summer, $100 to $115. Suites: fall/spring, $120 to $150; winter, $150 to $215; summer, $130 to $185.
Credit Cards:	All major
Remarks:	Children welcome. No pets.

When the boys saw John Colter belly up to the bar, they knew they were in for some tall tales. Often as not, he'd ramble on about his river roamin' days with Lewis and Clark. But if he every got around to that long-winded tale about heading south from the expedition only to come up on a devil's cauldtron of boiling sulfur fountains, thunderous waterfalls, gushing geysers and bison big as woolly mammoths, they'd end up laughing all the way home.

"Colter's Hell" may have been a pretty good joke back in the early 1800s, but it was John who got the last laugh. His "fanciful" account is now accepted as an accurate portrayal of the real-life wonders of Yellowstone National Park.

Historic Jackson Hole

The Hayden Expedition set out for northwest Wyoming in 1871 to explore the reputed Hades of the Western world. William Henry Jackson, a renowned photographer and Thomas Moran, the painter, were not prepared for what they saw: a land of awesome yet volatile beauty that would one day be known as Yellowstone and a chain of rugged peaks surrounding a heavenly valley, to be called Jackson Hole. But the admiration of the two explorers soon gave way to creative inspiration and they set to work capturing the true spirit of an incomparable landscape.

We all know how that story ends. Yellowstone would be preserved as America's first national park. The Tetons' stunning scenery would also win national park status. And Jackson Hole, a high alpine vally severed by the Snake river and dramatically enclosed by five mountain ranges, would provide the ideal setting for a colorful and inviting Western town.

A Landmark Meeting Place

The Wort Hotel has stood as a stalwart example of Jackson's enduring pride and spirit. Small in size, but big on Western hospitality (some of its staff have

been with the hotel for 30 and 40 years), it mirrors the atmosphere Jackson has become famous for, and with its convenient townsquare location, you are only steps away from all the activity of this cultural and recreational paradise.

A triple-A rated, four-Diamond hotel, The Wort offers 60 newly refurbished guest rooms and suites which feature traditional comfort with a decidely Western flair. All the custom-designed furnishings use only premium textiles and leather. Each room includes either a king or two double queen beds, television, telephone and full bath, as well as luxurious extras such as turn-down service in the evening and complete food and beverage room service. There's also a professional concierge to assist you in making the arrangements for all of your activities.

The Wort has also gained a reputation as a premier meeting and conference facility. Specializing in personalized service for groups of up to 100, the hotel boasts three separate conference rooms and several meeting suites, as well as state of the art audio-visual services. It books only one conference at a time to ensure that each group receives the full attention that it deserves.

2,032 and Counting

With a Western ambiance "as heavy as the fragrance of sagebrush," the Wort Hotel's famed Silver Dollar Bar and Grill is a favorite night spot and eatery . Exactly 2,032 brand new 1921 silver dollars are embeded in its bar top. And the regulars tell a wonderful story about the fire that broke out and the panic that ensued to save, not the building, but the silver dollar bar. The effort paid off and the renovation that followed has added both comfort and pizazz to a piece of Jackson's heritage.

But people don't just go out to eat and drink in these parts. Western Wyoming is Western swing country, and the lounge adjacent to the Silver Dollar Bar hosts the kind of live Country Western music that gets people on their feet and out on the floor. The Wort Cafe is a fine spot for a casual cup of coffee or a full meal, be it breakfast, after a late night of dancing, lunch or dinner.

From Cowboys to Concertos

Miles of wooden boardwalks guide you down Jackson's main streets and quaint Western facades mask the fact that many of the nation's most respected artisans now make their homes in Jackson Hole. Along with more than 80 restaurants, wildlife museums, specialty shops, three playhouses and night life that ranges from Country Western to jazz, you'll find no fewer than 40 art galleries featuring the works of outstanding artists. The Grand Teton Music Festival has for 28 seasons, proudly presented music to match our mountains. You'll also find the Old West Days celebration in May, the summer rodeo circuit, the famous Jackson Shootout which has been held every night for the past 33 years and daily stagecoach rides.

The Silver Dollar Bar adjoins the hotel.

Other activities include championship golf course as well as tennis, horseback riding and hot air ballooning. And you'll find whitewater and scenic float trips on the Snake River, windsurfing, waterskiing and fishing on alpine lakes.

Breathtaking scenery and dry Rocky Mountain powder are the hallmarks of the three excellent ski areas in Jackson Hole. The Jackson Hole Ski Resort is only twelve miles from The Wort. Grand Targhee with its tremendous powder and nonexistent crowds is 45 minutes away. And Snow King Mountain, so close that it casts a shadow over the town, is the perfect adventure for all skiers. Jackson Hole is also home to heli-skiing, miles of Nordic trails, ice skating, dog sledding and snowmobiling.

Getting There

The hotel is located just a half block off Town Square. Daily jet service connects Jackson Hole to most major cities. Complimentary shuttle to and from the hotel.

SPRING CREEK RESORT

Address:	P.O. Box 3154, Jackson, WY 83001
Telephone:	(307) 733-8833, (800) 443-6139
Host:	Vernon Johnson, General Manager
Room Rates:	Hotel rooms: spring/fall, $70 to $90; winter, $85 to $110; summer, $125 to $150.
	Condominiums: spring/fall, $100 to $220; winter, $100 to $285; summer, $135 to $360.
Credit Cards:	All major
Remarks:	Children welcome. No pets.

The panoramic landscape of Jackson Hole from the boiling Snake River up to the towering Tetons is a land of stubborn virtue. The low-lying valley and the mountains on high have always provided a sanctuary for elk, mule deer, bald eagles and hawks. And the people who came to the high desert respected the land and rejoiced in its beauty.

View with a Room

Spring Creek Resort, situated high atop East Gros Ventre Butte, 700 feet above the Jackson Hole Valley floor, encompasses 1,000 acres of breathtaking mountain views, superb facilities and Old West hospitality. Its creators spent both time and money making their plans blending the architecture with the environment and supervising every detail of construction.

The Resort's designers took the best of Jackson Hole's history and indigenous materials and formed them into a "drama that mirrors the beauty of the natural setting." Using rough-sawn timbers of fir and poles hewn from spruce and lodgepole pine, they created the Spring Creek Inn, the resort's four-star hotel and the Harvest Dance Lodges so that they would be rugged yet secluded. With unobtrusive exteriors of rough-cut red cedar, the buildings fade into the aspen and fir that grow on the hillsides. The guests see little sign of man's hand – they note, instead, the clouds that roll across the Wyoming sky, changing the sunset from red-orange to a deep shade of purple.

Sophistication and Solitude

Every one of the resort's 36 guest rooms and 62 luxurious condominiums take full advantage of the property's exhilarating views of the Tetons. Each unit's interior exemplifies the comfortable character of country, with rustically elegant lodgepole furniture, soft, muted colors and Indian prints and tapestries. You may also find living rooms with dramatic open ceilings that expose rough

timbers, bay windows, stained glass, towers, private balconies, window seats and nooks around stone fireplaces in a living room or master bedroom. Floors are wood planks and walls are hand-troweled, creating an atmosphere in which you can feel comfortable whether you're entertaining formally or wearing cowboy boots.

The amenities include remote-control cable television, refrigerators, terry robes, turn-down service and full kitchens even in the resort's studio and condominium units. The concierge is on call to arrange recreational activities for every season of the year and complimentary shuttle service is provided to and from the airport.

Under the grand Teton sky, guests of The Granary Restaurant can indulge in both the culinary and natural wonders of the Spring Creek Resort. The creative talents of master chefs present a delicious selection of international and American favorites for breakfast, lunch and dinner. During summer months, you can dine out on the deck, and a full bar and lounge provide a tranquil moment from a day of adventure and discovery.

With its first-class conference facilities, Spring Creek provides the perfect setting for board meetings, retreats and other executive gatherings. The three conference rooms and several meeting suites can accommodate groups of up to 140 and offer complete audio-visual services. And an outdoor area off the conference center provides the perfect scenic counterpart for social activities.

A Whirl with Recreation

Framed by nature's pure, unspoiled beauty, the Spring Creek Resort is like a candy store filled to the brim with sweet seasonal selections. In the summer, Ward Whitman heads up a professional team of wranglers at the resort's riding stables. There's tennis, hiking, swimming and an outdoor jacuzzi available. Two 18-hole championship courses are just minutes away. The ride on the aerial tram up Rendezvous Mountain's 10,500 foot peak, presents the valley and mountains at their panoramic best. Or you can ride a toboggan down Snow King Mountains Alpine Slide without a speck of snow in sight. Mountain climb among the giants in Grand Teton or Yellowstone National Park, or relax during a trip down a scenic river.

Jackson Hole is an artist's colony in every sense. Under the baton of Ling Tung, the Grand Teton Music Festival gets underway every July. The superb orchestra presents classical and modern concerts.

With winter, comes the thrill of Rocky Mountain powder. Three first-class ski areas — Jackson Hole Ski Resort (with the longest vertical drop of any mountain in North America), Grand Targhee (famous for its deep powder), and Snow King Ski Area — offer slopes for all ability levels. The Spring Creek

The Granary Restaurant has spectacular views of the Tetons.

bus drivers stop at the Targhee Express or Snow King bus stops in Jackson and drive directly to the slopes at Jackson Hole Ski Area.

The National Elk Refuge borders the resort and visitors who take the winter sleigh rides or wagons have an up-close view of the 8,000 head herd. Learn the art of dog sledding from Frank Teasley, the resort's full-fledged professional, and let the resort's nordic director show you why he's so enthused about the cross-country ski trails that wind through willow thickets and open meadows. And then top off a winter white day with a sleigh-taxi ride to and from a romantic evening at The Granary.

Getting There

The Spring Creek Ranch is approximately three miles north of Jackson. Take Highway 22 to Spring Gulch Road, then follow it north about a mile to the gate. Once through, continue up the hill another two and one-half miles to the resort. Jackson Airport is eight miles from the resort. They provide complimentary shuttle service.

THE BRIGHAM STREET INN

Address: 1135 East South Temple, Salt Lake City, UT 84102
Telephone: (801) 364-4461
Hosts: John and Nancy Pace
Room Rates: One single room, $65; double occupancy guest rooms, $85 to $95; suite with kitchen, $140. Rates include continental breakfast and afternoon tea.
Credit Cards: American Express, MasterCard, Visa
Remarks: Children over 12 welcome by arrangement. No pets.

"Where there's a will, there's a way," is something mothers usually say during our long-faced moments. But John and Nancy Pace had the will – a longing for a Victorian relic built for Water Cogswell Lyne in 1898. Thus, John midway through his morning shave suddenly asked, "What would you think of opening a bed and breakfast inn?" Nancy was speechless – that particular way had never crossed her mind.

Brigham Young's Era

At a board meeting of the Utah Heritage Foundation on which she served, Nancy found the means to perform the transformation. The foundation was contemplating several sites for a future designers' showcase. The Lyne House was a perfect candidate. One of the last remaining mansions of Brigham Young's era, its beauty had faded through years of disuse and abuse. But the deadline was a hand – completion was required in four months' time. The Paces accepted the challenge and took the plunge. The foundation would use the house for the first month after the showcase opening for fundraising, after which it would become one of Salt Lake City's first bed and breakfast inns.

A Star is Born

With a 12-member American Society of Interior Designers team, the Paces went to work with excitement and enthusiasm. From the rubble of an alcoholic rehabilitation center emerged an elegant, yet contemporary inn. Its grace and style won not only the awards of architectural masters, but the hearts of all who entered its doors.

Set on a corner among the chestnut trees and red sandstone sidewalks of South Temple Street, the 2 1/2 story, red brick mansion is still the part-Classical Revival, part-Queen Anne Victorian it was when first occupied by Walter Lyne, a prosperous Presbyterian wool broker and his family. Once inside you'll find another world. To quiet the flamboyance of its Victorian past, John and Nancy decided to emphasize the house's sense of timelessness.

"It's definitely not the austere man's home I remember," says Walter Lyne's granddaughter, Virginia, who flew her private plane from Wyoming to visit the Paces in the midst of renovation. She was amazed at the changes. Her grandfather's unfinished attic library, with its slanted ceilings, dormers and skylights had been converted into three spacious guest rooms, which look out over the lights of the valley. Nine and one-half baths were added and the servant's basement had become a romantic suite. It had even had a name change. Named for the most prestigious boulevard in Salt Lake, Brigham Street Inn, the Paces welcomed their first guests in May 1982.

The Appealing Aspects

The inn combines the most appealing aspects of a bed and breakfast with those of a luxury hotel. Each of the nine guest rooms has a private bath, telephone and color television. You'll find the brilliance of fresh flowers through the inn, turndown bed service at night and a newspaper every morning. Five of the rooms have cozy fireplaces and all are decorated with impeccable taste.

The inn's only suite was no more than a desolate basement prior to the renovation. Located at garden level, it has its own private entrance with a living room, kitchen, bedroom and huge bath. This self-contained suite is perfect for larger families or private honeymooners.

If you believe that people should dominate the room, rather than the room dominate the people, you'll appreciate the Inn's parlor. The delicately carved bird's eye maple fireplace, the light furnishings and carpeting offer a homey, pleasant background for conversation and a perfect setting for small meetings. The living room, in comparison, has bold walls, a white ceiling and golden oak floors, shutters and moldings. A lustrous black ebony piano, set against a lovely beveled window, often steals the spotlight during afternoon tea. And the dining room presided over with aplomb by Hector the rabbit, sports a light, fresh look with its splashes of blue and beige, a gorgeous oak and tile fireplace and large hunt table. Nancy's continental buffet breakfast is both elegant and satisfying.

Salt Lake — A Sensational City

The Brigham Street Inn's location is smack dab in the center of the city. Just minutes away is Temple Square, which provides visitors with a magnificent overview of Mormon history. You can walk through the beauty of the Temple, find your genealogical roots at the Family History Library, and witness the inspired pride of the city's founding fathers. The University of Utah is close by and its ongoing musical, theatrical and education events provide Salt Lake residents and tourists with many memorable performances.

The dining room is a splendid place to enjoy breakfast.

If you prefer the thrill of athleticism and braving the elements, there are no less than seven outstanding ski areas in the hollows of Salt Lake's numerous canyons. Park City, Deer Valley, Snowbird, Alta, Solitude – their names form the essence of the legendary light Utah power and their slopes try the skill and endurance of even the most avid skier.

Salt Lake, although restricted to set-ups and wine service due to stringent liquor laws, plays host to a number of wonderful first class establishments.

Getting There

Take Interstate 80 into Salt Lake City. As you near the airport downtown, take the North Temple exit and drive east approximately two miles to State Street. Turn right one block to South Temple and turn left. Go east on South Temple 11 blocks to R Street. The Brigham Street Inn is on the corner of R and South Temple. There is a parking lot around the back of the inn.

THE HOMESTEAD

Address:	P.O. Box 99, 700 N. Homestead Drive, Midway, UT 84049
Telephone:	(801) 654-1102/649-2060, for Utah reservations (800) 327-7220, for out-of-state reservations
Hosts:	Jerry and Carole Sanders, owners
Room Rates:	Honeymoon suites and luxury rooms: $79 to $150. Double, includes continental breakfast. Guest rooms: $59 to $79 double
Credit Cards:	American Express, MasterCard, Visa
Remarks:	Children welcome. No pets.

"I hate to write about a place I am fond of, because I make it sound too good, I may encourage other people to overrun and improve it." Wallace Stegner wrote these words more than 30 years ago to describe his beloved Heber Valley. And Stegner would be startled to know that his words are as true of the pristine valley today as they were 30 years ago.

For there remains a place unchanged by time, a place with shaded lanes, formal flower gardens and manicured lawns, where gentlefolk continue to enjoy life in refined comfort. A place where a thick carpeting of lush green grass still covers the valley, where 12,000-foot Mt. Timpanogos remains the master of an unspoiled domain. A place known today as, The Homestead.

From Hot Pots to Hospitality

The thrill of land and a farm of his own brought a Morman settler, Simon Schneitter, into the Heber Valley. And as he began to till the soil in anticipation of planting, he uncovered hot springs and mineral rock deposits. Simon, an industrious man, soon reasoned that trading in his plow for an innkeeper's cap was the only sensible thing to do. With his wife Fanny's blessings and her good cooking, Simon opened The Schneitter Family Hotel and Hot Pots in 1910.

The Schneitters began a tradition of hospitality. On a cold winter evening guests could expect an evening of good cheer. With warm greetings, Simon would take coats and hats, ushering friends out of the cold, into a house so crisp and clean that the blues and whites sparkled and the hardwoods shone.

Keeping Traditions Alive

It is a scene that fueled Jerry and Carole Sanders' desire to purchase the 60 acres of property in 1986 and renovate the classic two-story early American

Hotel, as well as its seven outbuildings. Two years and five million dollars of thoughtful and detailed work later, the first phase of the new Homestead shines as warm and comforting as the old. The second phase of the expansion is well underway, with an 18-hole golf course, riding stables, tennis courts and swimming pool planned to meet the needs of the visitors who will occupy the 50 new guest rooms and suites.

The original seven houses and cottages spread out amid spring-fed creeks and meadows. They now include 83 rooms and can accommodate from one to ten guests each. Mingled in with turn-of-the-century antiques, brass lamps and hand-painted porcelain sinks and shower heads are all the modern conveniences of a resort hotel in a country setting. The Guest House, which features a luxurious bedroom with an antique king-size bed, separate parlor with fireplace and huge bath with a mirrored tub for two, is ideal for honeymooning. And the more informal rooms in The Barn, furnished with two queen beds and a bunk room off to the side, are perfect for larger families.

Home, Sweet Homestead

"I want to feel like we're talking to friends, not guests," says Jerry. So it is not uncommon to find Jerry or Carole stopping to chat with old and new friends in the relaxing Homestead dining room. There, Chef Robert Harper creates a variety of culinary delights for breakfast, lunch and dinner.

A large indoor and outdoor pool, whirlpool, sauna and soothing nonsulfuric hot mineral baths are available for guests year round. Incurable romantics can enjoy private use of The Virginia House's hot tub and solarium, and order continental breakfast in its sunstreamed quiet. Five first-class meeting and banquet rooms provide conference facilities for groups of 20 to 120 people. And Whimsey's Gift Shop is filled with memorabilia and delicacies such as cream and butter fudge to appeal to your sweet tooth.

Recreation Destination

The Homestead is clearly an uncommon country resort. It is also a playground for visitors. Springtime ushers in long days of outdoor activities. Tennis, croquet, volleyball, shuffleboard and horseshoes hone your competitive skills. The magnificent trails of the Wasatch Mountains are open to horseback riding, as well as hiking and mountain bicycling. Until The Homestead completes its own 18-hole championship golf course (making it the only golf resort in Utah), the Wasatch Mountain State Golf Course is only 1/2 mile down the road. Nearby Strawberry and Deer Creek reservoirs offer fishing and boating and the Provo River represents some of America's finest flyfishing waters. Hay rides and the Heber Creeper railroad take you through an assortment of low altitude beauty, and hot air balloons and helicopter flights provide spectacular rides over many famous peaks and ski areas.

The beautiful grounds are ideal for walking.

The Homestead has with the addition of its own cross country ski center at the Wasatch Mountain State Park only 1/2 mile away been billed as "Park City's newest ski resort." The summer pro shop doubles as a winter chalet complete with a PSIA ski school. At the chalet, rental and retail shops provide the professional services needed so that skiers of all abilities can enjoy the miles of track that cross the varied terrain. Alpine enthusiasts have a choice of four great ski areas with a 19-mile radius – Deer Valley, Park City West, Park City and Robert Redford's creation, Sundance. Heli-skiing, ice fishing, sleigh rides and guided snowmobile tours are also options for winter fun.

Getting There

From Interstate 80, drive south on U.S. 40 past Park City a few miles to a sign that reads "Midway, one mile." Turn west toward the mountains, go through the town of Midway and follow the signs to The Homestead, which is about one and one-half mile out of town.

SPECIAL INDEXES

	Restaurant open to the public	No. of people for meeting facilities	Kitchens available in some rooms	Fireplaces in some rooms	Facilities for the handicapped	Spas or hot tubs available	Swimming pool on premises	Tennis on premises	Golf available	Horses available	Boating available	Fishing on premises	Children under 12 welcome	Spectacular views
California														
Inn at Rancho Santa Fe	●	120		●			●	●	●				●	
Little Inn on the Bay		25					●				●	●	●	
Villa Rosa		18	●	●		●	●						●	
The Alisal Guest Ranch		150		●		●	●	●	●	●	●	●	●	●
The Martine Inn		24		●	●	●								●
The Babbling Brook				●										
Inn at the Opera	●	80	●		●								●	
The Spencer House														
The Mansion at Lakewood		60		●		●	●							
The Wine Country Inn				●		●	●							●
The Foothill House				●										
The Toll House				●	●	●								
Whale Watch Inn by the Sea			●	●		●						●		●
The Stanford Inn by the Sea		20	●	●							●	●	●	●
Benbow Inn	●	20		●		●					●	●	●	
Gingerbread Mansion				●										
Carter House/Hotel Carter	●	10		●		●							●	
Pacific Northwest														
Paradise Ranch Inn	●	50	●			●		●	●		●	●	●	●
Black Butte Ranch Lodge	●	35	●	●		●	●	●	●	●		●	●	●
Rock Springs Ranch		50	●	●		●	●	●		●		●	●	
RiverPlace Alexis Hotel	●	200	●	●	●	●	●				●	●	●	●
Heron Haus							●							●
Heathman Hotel	●	150											●	
Columbia Gorge Hotel	●	200	●	●									●	●
The Shelburne Inn	●	50		●									●	
Alexis Hotel Seattle	●	75	●	●	●			●					●	
The Inn at the Market		70			●	●							●	●
Home by the Sea		14	●	●	●	●					●	●		
Inn at Langley	●	30		●	●	●						●		●
The Saratoga Inn														●
Turtleback Farm Inn												●		
Inn at Semiahmoo	●	770		●	●	●	●	●	●		●	●	●	●

	Restaurant open to the public	No. of people for meeting facilities	Kitchens available in some rooms	Fireplaces in some rooms	Facilities for the handicapped	Spas or hot tubs available	Swimming pool on premises	Tennis on premises	Golf available	Horses available	Boating available	Fishing on premises	Children under 12 welcome	Spectacular views	Pets welcome
stern Canada															
Bedford Hotel	●	100		●	●	●								●	
gail's Hotel				●		●									
consfield Inn				●		●									
ke Harbour House	●	50		●		●						●		●	
stings House	●	14		●		●			●		●	●		●	
il Point Lodge	●	120		●		●					●	●	●	●	
k Royal Hotel	●	50												●	
heume Lake Resort		20		●							●	●	●		
erald Lake Lodge	●	120	●	●	●	●				●	●	●		●	
falo Mountain Lodge	●	120	●	●	●	●				●			●	●	
thern Rockies															
er Street Inn						●									●
sterback Ranch	●	20				●				●	●	●	●	●	
dahar Lodge		50	●			●							●	●	
head Lake Lodge		150					●	●		●	●	●	●	●	
e Mountain Ranch	●	60		●		●				●			●	●	
untain Sky Guest Ranch		75		●		●	●	●		●		●	●	●	
Wort Hotel	●	100											●		
ing Creek Resort	●	140		●		●	●	●					●	●	
Brigham Street Inn				●											
Homestead	●	120		●	●	●	●	●	●	●	●	●	●		

TO REORDER

If you would like to re-order additional copies of *Special Places*, please use the attached mailing card. If the card has already been used, send your name, address and $14.95 plus $1.50 for postage and handling to:

Special Places, Inc.
P.O. Box 378
Issaquah, WA 98027
(206) 392-0451

PLEASE HELP!

Your reactions to the Special Places in this book are very important to us. Please complete one of the attached post cards after you experience one of the Special Places. We will use the information you provide to help us in the on-going process of monitoring the quality and service of each place listed in this book.

Something Special for You

Each time you send in a postcard (or a letter if you choose) we will enter your name in a Quarterly drawing. One prize will be awarded in each of four random drawings in January, April, July, and October. *The prize will be two nights lodging in the Special Place of your choice.* To be eligible, entrants must be 21 years of age.

Discoveries You Feel Are Special?

If during your travels you discover a place you feel is quite special, we would appreciate you letting us know. Any suggestions in the 13 western states and two western Canadian provinces will be investigated.

Thanks
Fred and Mardi

Special Places

for the discerning traveler

Please send me _____ copies of SPECIAL PLACES® at $14.95 each, plus $1.50 for shipping and handling. Send to:

NAME

ADDRESS

CITY

STATE   ZIP

In

CALIFORNIA, THE PACIFIC NORTHWEST

WESTERN CANADA AND

THE NORTHERN ROCKIES

Special Places

Dear Fred and Mardi,

We experienced the following Special Place: _____

on _____   (Reservation date) and have these comments:

_____

_____

_____

Free Drawing

Enter me in the free quarterly drawing.

Name

Address   City   State/Zip

New Discoveries

We discovered a place we feel is Special and think you should see:

_____

_____

Special Places

P.O. Box 378

Issaquah, WA 98027

Special Places

P.O. Box 378

Issaquah, WA 98027

Special Places

for the discerning traveler

Please send me _____ copies of SPECIAL PLACES® at $14.95 each, plus $1.50 for shipping and handling. Send to:

_____
NAME

_____
ADDRESS

_____
CITY

_____
STATE   ZIP

In

CALIFORNIA, THE PACIFIC NORTHWEST

WESTERN CANADA AND

THE NORTHERN ROCKIES

Special Places

Dear Fred and Mardi,

We experienced the following Special Place: _____

on _____ (Reservation date) and have these comments:

_____

_____

_____

Free Drawing

Enter me in the free quarterly drawing.

_____
Name

_____
Address   City   State/Zip

New Discoveries

We discovered a place we feel is Special and think you should see:

_____

_____

Special Places
P.O. Box 378
Issaquah, WA 98027

Special Places
P.O. Box 378
Issaquah, WA 98027